Parenting Adhd

Overcoming the Deceptions that Shackle Parents

(How to Raise an Emotionally Healthy Child)

Lonnie Devault

Published by Rob Miles

© **Lonnie Devault**

All Rights Reserved

Parenting Adhd: Overcoming the Deceptions that Shackle Parents (How to Raise an Emotionally Healthy Child)

ISBN 9781990084423

All rights reserved. No part of this guide may be reproduced in any form without permission in writing from the publisher except in the case of brief quotations embodied in critical articles or reviews.

Legal & Disclaimer

The information contained in this book is not designed to replace or take the place of any form of medicine or professional medical advice. The information in this book has been provided for educational and entertainment purposes only.

The information contained in this book has been compiled from sources deemed reliable, and it is accurate to the best of the Author's knowledge; however, the Author cannot guarantee its accuracy and validity and cannot be held liable for any errors or omissions. Changes are periodically made to this book. You must consult your doctor or get professional medical advice before using any of the suggested remedies, techniques, or information in this book.

Upon using the information contained in this book, you agree to hold harmless the Author from and against any damages, costs, and expenses, including any legal fees potentially resulting from the application of any of the information provided by this guide. This disclaimer applies to any damages or injury caused by the use and application, whether directly or indirectly, of any advice or information presented, whether for breach of contract, tort, negligence, personal injury, criminal intent, or under any other cause of action.

You agree to accept all risks of using the information presented inside this book. You need to consult a professional medical practitioner in order to ensure you are both able and healthy enough to participate in this program.

Table of Contents

INTRODUCTION 1

CHAPTER 1: BEHAVIORAL AND EMOTIONAL DISTRESS 5

CHAPTER 2: TIME OUT THAT WORKS 9

CHAPTER 3: MOBILITY 27

CHAPTER 4: SPENDING PRIME TIME TOGETHER 34

CHAPTER 5: PARENTING PITFALLS 40

CHAPTER 6: DISCIPLINING YOUR CHILD 45

CHAPTER 7 50

CHAPTER 8: WHAT IS THE TERRIBLE TWOS? 53

CHAPTER 9: WHAT IS PARENTING ALL ABOUT? 62

CHAPTER 10: BEING A SINGLE PARENT DOES NOT MEAN RAISING AN UNSTABLE CHILD 68

CHAPTER 11: THE PARENT GAME 74

CHAPTER 12: CATEGORISE 78

CHAPTER 13: ENCOURAGEMENT AND PRAISE MAKE YOUR CHILD FEEL IMPORTANT 84

CHAPTER 14: PROPER COMMUNICATION 90

CHAPTER 15: AGE GROUPS AND ISSUES 94

CHAPTER 16: SEVEN WAYS TO SPEND TIME WITH YOUR KIDS 101

CHAPTER 17: STEP DAD OR STEPPED ON DAD 106

CHAPTER 18: MAKING NEW FRIENDS 108

CHAPTER 19: FINANCIAL LITERACY.WHAT SHOULD YOU TEACH YOUR CHILD? 114

CHAPTER 20: POWER OF POSITIVE PARENTING............. 123

CHAPTER 21: WHY WE 'NEVER' DISCIPLINE OUR CHILDREN 129

CHAPTER 22: BUILDING RESILIENT CHILDREN................ 139

CHAPTER 23: TEENAGE SEX AND CONTRACEPTION 144

CHAPTER 24: PARENTING STYLES 156

CHAPTER 25: ESCAPING THE MADNESS 166

CHAPTER 26: VISITATIONS AND DIVORCE...................... 172

CHAPTER 27: WHAT FACTORS INFLUENCE THE PARENTING PHILOSOPHY OF PARENT? 181

CHAPTER 28: BULLY STRATEGIES: TEACH YOUR CHILD HOW TO DEAL WITH BULLIES 184

CHAPTER 29: ALWAYS HAVE A REASON 187

CONCLUSION 191

Introduction

Most parents will agree with me that raising a smart kid can be quite challenging. There are many loopholes in nurturing smartness in a kid, and while you may succeed in bringing out the best in him/her, there might be a possibility of the child lacking in other areas of life. You may have heard a parent say, "My kid is smart; but..." Sounds familiar, right? Well, the reason why this happens is that focusing on one area of a child's life tends to cause an imbalance in the other parts of their life. Many parents report their children having some sort of discontent in one way or the other. For instance, a bright child may be successful in school while struggling to fit in with their peers, or is obsessed with perfectionism. On the other hand, others may find it hard dealing with failure because they are used to being high achievers, or may lack the zeal to try something out of fear of failure.

These scenarios are common among many children. If you are not careful, you may end up with a smart kid who is lacking in self-empathy. The trick is to strike a balance in all aspects of your child's life from childhood.

There are numerous speculations as to the development of a child's brain. Some people believe that the first three years are the most crucial in nurturing a child's ability. Others believe that this is the time you are supposed to let your child just be a child. So who is right? While it is true that the right time to nurture a child's ability is in his early years, it does not mean that the child cannot learn the abilities later on in life. Unlike popular believe, the brain of a child continues to grow through adolescence and well into adulthood. Therefore, with the exception of a few cases, chances are high that you can nurture your child's abilities from an early stage all the way through adolescence. Some of the cases that are fool proof with this scenario include language and patterned visual information. If you do not expose your child to language in the first year of his life, it is highly likely that he/she will not use it correctly. Similarly, failure to expose your child to patterned visual information at an early age may render the child incapable of developing normal depth perception. However, it is important to note that a few factors may influence your child's ability to learn. For starters, a child's ability to learn new skills is highly influenced by genetics. Not everyone can become Michael Jordan, no matter how early you start teaching the child basketball. Everyone is born with a different ability that can be developed only so far no matter your experiences. Secondly, as said earlier, while it is true that the first years of a child's life are crucial for their development, it does not mean that they are doomed to failure and mediocrity if certain experiences do not occur.

Chapter 1: Behavioral And Emotional Distress

There are several reason why being a single parenting is a bad idea, there are the obvious reasons, and the deeper reasons that most people do not think about when they enter into becoming a single parent.Being a single parent brings with it many struggles for both the parents embarking on that road, and the children that are involved without their consent.

The struggle for financial stability is in the most part a never-ending battle.Many single parents are on government assistance or have to work whatever job, shift and hours available to accommodate their family's needs.It is a difficult life to balance and of course, even if you have the financial means to sustain a single income family there is the inability to adequately meet the needs of your children.Time, energy and physical presence is divided between other children, and the single parent, leaving most single parents exhausted, and frustrated.

Then of course are the damning statistics that voice against single parenting and that list runs long and one of those items on that lengthy list is how both the single parent and the child or the children are affected by anxiety and stress.Studies have shown that single parent households are under a tremendous more amount of stress than households with two parents.We live in a time where stress among people and families is already seeing intense thresholds, and the reality of that stress is compounded with the family that is run by a single parent.

For the children involved, they too bare a lot of stress and when that stress accumulates it leads to a variety of behavioral and emotional problems.There is a much higher subjectivity of behavioral and emotional distress.If the situation is a new situation, many kids do not have an ability to adequately adjust. And that is to be expected, parents have a difficult time adjusting so why would people expect to see anything less from their children.Children that are subject to a new single parent environment often become confused, lonely, fearful, sad and angry and these emotion are often unleashed in very negative ways.

Children that have been brought up in a single parent environment since their birth may be adjusted to the family dynamic, however, they too experience high amounts of stress andbehavioral disorders that stem from abandonment issues, neglect, inability to cope and other forceful stressors in the home.

In addition to the children that are under stress in a single parent household, the parent involved is typically highly stressed as well.The responsibility of being both mother and father, financial provider, car pool, chaperone, disciplinarian, teacher, emotional strength and so many other hats that a single parent wears can only add to their stress level.And, when a parent becomes stressed, that will spill over on the children as well, creating a dynamic of stress among the entire household.

This is not to say that children of duo parent systems do not experience stress, nor to the parents, however, the studies and statistics have shown that the levels of stress, emotional and behavioral disorders are extreme in single parent households.

Chapter 2: Time Out That Works

I want to emphasize that when used correctly to stop a behavior, Time Out is an effective tool for bringing peace and calm into life.The danger is that when Time Out is not used correctly, it is very easy to slip into punishment not discipline.What I will teach in this section is based on Time Out theories and my behavioral theory, The Emotional Arousal Cycle.Once you learn to use it correctly, Time Out is an effective and appropriate method of gaining control of a life and opening pathways to change. For the benefit of my children, I will also add that NO, I did not always do this correctly. YES, I have grown, and I am sorry for having to learn these things through you.I think you turned out pretty well, in spite of my mistakes, and these readers thank you for your sacrifice.

What Time Out is NOT

Time Out IS NOT PUNISHMENT.In fact, the fastest route to peace and joy in parenting comes when you stop punishing and start disciplining.However, even a well-executed Time Out can be very quickly become punishing if the one imposing the Time Out is not careful.

For clarification, Punishment and Discipline are not synonymous.At its root, punishment means the infliction of pain, or to make one pay, whereas the root meaning of discipline is to teach.As parents, our fullest joy comes from teaching our children a better way and helping them gain the discipline to be self governing.Can there be a more satisfying moment than when a child takes control of a situation and self-regulates based on the principles you have been working so hard to teach?Only through discipline is this transfer of self control accomplished.Punishment has never had the power to change behavior in the same way discipline can.And really, how do you want to be remembered, as a fearsome and dark punisher, or as a nurturing and supportive disciplinarian?

My introduction to Time Out was while working in an agency for troubled youth, and as I have grown in my knowledge of the process, as well as my understanding of the brain/body/emotion connection in times of chaos and stress, I now recognize that on numerous occasions we unknowingly crossed the line between discipline and punishment. Some time ago, while working a trade show, I was in a booth directly across from some folks who had made some very nice child-sized chairs, attractively tole-painted with various TIME OUT CHAIR titles. I am sure that they were intended to be cute, but a couple of them had very demeaning, labeling, and shaming statements. One simply said, "The Naughty Chair".Okay, that one is not too bad.The message "I Am Naughty" on another, however, carried a much more shame- and blame-based message.Such labeling tips the scale from discipline to punishment and creates a mental view of self that can be very hard to overcome.Along this same line, Time Out is also NOT abandonment to a dark room, the child's room, or some other isolated corner, because as an intervention, it quickly loses any chance for nurture when the caregiver is not present.Instead, you can maximize Time Out's effectiveness by being present in the process and seeking opportunity to nurture as soon as the chance shows itself. But during the process of correction, if the child feels abandoned or shamed, the window for self-doubt and internal ridicule is thrown wide open.

While teaching these concepts, I have heard a broad range of Time Out definitions and techniques.Generally, such discussion of "What is a Time Out?" incorporates some form of isolation, an uncomfortable position, and—in some cases—a form of humiliation, similar to the (thankfully) long-lost "Dunce Cap."

Additionally, inflicting pain on the child weakens your ability to discipline from a nurturing position. When your child is isolated and alone, there is no chance for nurture, and subsequently, you miss a critical moment of emotional refraction (see Emotional Arousal Cycle Graphic, below).

In order to maintain a positive and joyful experience as a parent and to create a learning environment for the child, Time Out should be free of any type of physical discomfort and pain. Some have been so stern as to not allow the child to move at all or they would make it longer or tack on more penalty. But take a moment to examine yourself: even now, as an adult, are YOU able to sit stock still? Even if you are able to remain stone-still, are your able to if at the same time you are emotionally and physically agitated? Of course not, so why do we believe that a five-year-old can?Allowing yourself to become emotionally upset, or challenged, by the child who is doing what is physically, developmentally, and emotionally appropriate while in a time out is like taking the fast track to frustration.

I have heard terrible stories from clients talking about Time Out being a painful experience where they had to have their nose on the wall while they stood on tiptoe.One acquaintance described being forced to do Time Out in an "air-chair" position on the wall or in the push-up bridge position.Such postures during Time Out are punishing, and constitute demoralization for the child.This type of parental interaction is self-gratifying to the needs of the adult inflicting the punishment.Ultimately, it will lead to despair and frustration as the parent—the opposite of what this guide can help you achieve.

Time Out is also NOT discipline by itself.

Rather, it is part of a larger discipline action. When used appropriately, Time Out prepares you and the child to engage in the most critical element: disciplinary teaching that will create change. Trying to effectively this change could be why we even decided to tangle with the child in the first place. The goal of any Time Out action is to get the child redirected, calmed, and ready to receive instruction. It is also for you, the parent and adult, to maintain your calm, ask yourself the three questions, and decide why the situation rose to such a level of arousal that a TIME Out was required. Failure to do this creates nothing more than punishment for a behavior. The child needs to be assisted in understanding three things;

1. WHY you, the Disciplinarian, felt a Time Out was needed

2. WHAT the Time Out is intended to do

3. HOW a Time Out can be avoided in the future by choosing a better action.

When the child has internalized these three fundamental rules, they will be able to self-direct.This then frees you the parent to enjoy your time teaching and playing, since you will not be so crisis focused and crazed with out-of-control kids.

What IS Time Out, and WHY??

Time Out is -

An effective method of stopping undesired behavior,

collecting your thoughts, and allowing the child to calm down

so that teaching can occur.

Effectively used, Time Out will prepare the opportunity to teach while redirecting the child's behavior from the thing that is creating the negative arousal.It keeps you calm and relaxed because you will be able to sort through your own emotions before and during the Time Out. In sports, time out is used very strategically and the teams are only allowed a few time outs per game.Coaches or team captains will use the time out to regroup, to slow the game, or to stop a run by the opposing team.We need to see Time Out with our children (and for our self) the same way.A Time Out is used to stop the behavior and redirect the action.Then, like a coach does during a time out, you huddle with the child. You guide and nurture while giving instruction.If Time Out is used as your only intervention it will quickly lose its effectiveness.I had a roommate once who was spanked daily.He talked about how that lost any impact as well. To maintain Time Out's effectiveness as much as possible, use it like a sports coach: with skill and careful timing, while also utilizing other proactive methods in less demanding moments.All too often, Time Out is seen as a chance for the parent to check out, instead of checking in.

Fundamentally, Time Out looks like this:

1.The child's behavior(s) escalate(s) to a point from which the child is unreachable through direct conversation or distraction. The parent specifically identifies the behavior which the child must engage in or cease, and then warns that a time out will be necessary if the child does not comply. However, be aware that in some cases, when the misbehavior is too dire, and immediate parental action must be taken. For example, physical aggression necessitates immediate response, just as referees immediately respond to a foul in a sporting event.

2. The parent asks herself the first question, "Why do I care that my child is doing this?" This is a very important self-assessment to conduct in order to be sure she is not reacting to something childish, or other inconsequential misbehavior. If the behavior is deemed to be a true misbehavior and not just something the adult finds to be personally annoying, a final warning is given in a calm, gentle manner.

3.The child is directed to a designated spot and informed that it is necessary to take a Time Out in order to work out what is going on. The reason for the Time Out is always based on a specific behavior and not personalized to the child as a character trait, "you were bad."

4.Instructions should be given as to how long the child will be there, and what the adult's role will be in the process.

These instructions ought to include:

-Directing the child to sit quietly in a specified location.

-Explanation that the time will not begin until the child is able to sit quietly (not still) and contemplate the action.

-Information about what you will be doing

-Specifics about how long the Time Out will be or what the child needs to do in order to show they have calmed completely.

Adapted from P.R.I.D.E. foster and adoptive parent training created by the Child Welfare League of America

When To Use Time Out

As I said before, just as in sports, there are only so many Time Outs you can use.Overused, Time Out loses its effectiveness.The last thing you want to do is to lose a good tool due to over use or using it in the wrong way.The graphic below comes from the authors work, The Emotional Arousal Cycle.It illustrates the various stages of mental and emotional functioning and how to assess where your child is, and when to use the Time Out.Once you learn the Emotional Arousal Cycle, you are equipped with the most effective assessment tool you need to change your child's behavior.

Reading the cycle is simple, but its impact is huge in creating your joyful experience in raising your child.The question "why do I care" is part of the Emotional Arousal assessment and when you ask it of yourself, you are able to remain in your full mental abilities without escalating to the state where you need the Time Out.

However, this is not a bad option at times. Please refer to the graphic of the Emotional Arousal Cycle below as you read the following information. The Emotional Arousal Cycle is the result of several years of research and observation with children and adults.Learning to read the emotional state of the child will allow you to gain a deeper control of the situation and respond in a more appropriate way. It gives you as the parent a way to approach.

The first level on the cycle shows the state of emotional normality that we experience in a non-stressed state of contentment.The movement of the emotional line represents gentle fluctuations in the daily emotional state.In this "normal" state the brain is in its full state of mental ability.The ability to rationalize and reason is fully engaged.It should be noted the rational mind is not fully developed until the early 20's.So the very act of reasoning with a child is often met with frustration.Prior to age 12, the child has very limited ability to conceptualize and look at the big picture.They are very concrete and much of their mental state is driven by emotion and physical need.If you let your adult mental capacity fall apart by getting emotionally aroused, you will lose the joy and happiness that is yours when you discipline with effective interventions.

The second level of arousal occurs in the limbic system of the middle brain. This part of the brain is all about emotion, alertness, and reaction.This is what senses danger and also shuts off the logic brain.Mushy, love-y teenagers are all limbic, and we know too well that there is little logic in most of that!When you are attuned to your child's play and begin to sense that there is a problem, it is the limbic system alerting you.It is at this point that the effective interventions shown in the right column can stop the escalation before it reaches Time Out stage. By staying fully relaxed and simply engaging the child by asking them to identify at least five feeling reflection words (emotional expression), expressing your own feelings, and getting the child to talk, you remain in a calm and controlled state and keep your child from further escalation.

The third level of arousal occurs in the most primitive part of the human brain-- the "reptilian core".This area is solely driven by survival instincts.When one of you—parent or child--escalates to this point, you are headed to a Time Out.The emotion of the limbic has closed off and the body and mind are focused solely on preservation.There is no reasoning. There is little variable emotion. There is only Fight/Flight (fueled by rage, anger, and adrenaline) or Freeze (that deer-in-the-headlights, stunned and overwhelmed look).In this involuntary state, called tonic immobility, the child's body goes completely limp and they appear calm, but they are actually in a mental/emotionally "dead" state in an attempt to have the threat pass them by.This "lifelessness" is a survival response and in no way a consciously chosen behavior. Getting upset that a child in this state is not engaging with you is pointless and will only lead to YOU needing a Time Out.

The "Frolic" referred to in the graphic is not generally seen in young kids, but is the very physical escalation that every parent fears when their teen goes out.It is the ultimate form of species preservation.

Time Out is intended to calm down the arousal cycle and get the logic brain to fully re-engage and allow for teaching in the moment of emotional refraction.That dip when the emotions are exhausted and normal status has not regained dominance.Being engaged, present, and nurturing during the entire process is one of the greatest moments you can have as a parent.

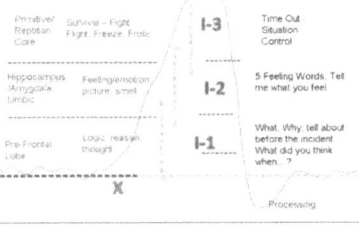

Emotional Arousal Cycle

Using the above graphic as a model, Time Out is employed ONLY when the situation has escalated to a point that the child has lost physical or emotional control and is in need of redirection and calming. Prior to the use of Time Out, the joyful parent will have used all other means of interventions to reach the child (further discussion of pre-Time Out interventions can be found in the author's work The Art and Joy of Parenting with Discipline for a Change). Time Out should ONLY be utilized when the child is too escalated and cannot be calmed through other means, because when aroused to this point, the child is full of adrenaline and is emotionally and mentally unavailable. Therefore, he needs to be removed from all stimulation and allowed to calm down. Other forms of engagement with him while in this time will only result in frustration for you and the potential for emotional harm to the child.

Chapter 3: Mobility

Babies are God's gifts and bring joy and happiness into the lives of parents. New parents are overjoyed at the prospect of adding a new member to the family and are typically enthusiastic about the addition. But the initial euphoria of having a baby dies down after a few months when parents realize how difficult it is to take care of newborns, especially without help.

It becomes an important task to think for babies, as they are incapable of thinking for themselves and frequently act out on impulse. They tend to take up activities that they think are fun without understanding what these actions can lead to. Now, as scary as that sounds, it is a fact and quite important for new parents to prepare themselves for the journey that lies ahead of them.

During the first few months, the onus lies on the parents to handle babies with care.

They will not be able to operate by themselves thereby necessitating 24-hour care. Parents tend to take turns tending to their babies and ensure that their newborn is comfortable and happy.

The real challenge begins when the baby starts becoming mobile. It is human nature to be curious and adventurous and babies tend to be both. As soon as they start crawling, they begin to explore around them. As parents, it becomes important to prepare for this eventuality and ensure that your baby has a safe environment to explore in the transition from baby to toddler.

This section looks at some of the things to expect and prepare for, while your toddler starts to crawl and walk.

Crawling

Most babies start to crawl by the age of 6 to 10 months. It is important for parents to keep an eye on their baby at all times to ensure that the home is prepared ready for the curiosity the child will display.

Crawling is an important stage of growth and it is quite important to let your baby learn to crawl freely. It will be up to you to create a safe environment for your baby and help him/her have fun while crawling.

The first step will be to ensure that your baby is placed inside a bed or crib that has high gates. This will ensure that your baby does not get out during the night when you are asleep or when you are not keeping an eye on him or her. How high the gates need to be will depend on the baby's height and how adventurous the baby is.

The next step will be to place barriers across staircases. This will ensure that your baby does not tumble out and over the stairs. Having a gate at the bottom of stairs as well as at the top is vital.

If you have a dedicated room for your baby then it will be best to cover up all the electric outlets. Babies tend to stick their fingers into these out of curiosity and this can prove to be highly dangerous. There are covers available from several different stores that are easy to install.

Ensure that there are no sharp objects on the floor where your baby crawls. A baby will not think before placing his/her hands and knees onto it, thereby endangering themselves. Placing a soft carpet on the floor will make sure your baby is comfortable.

Walking

Once the crawling stage passes, parents have to prepare for the walking stage. This is a little tougher to deal with as babies will become quite independent and start walking and running around.

This stage is just as important as the crawling stage and it is important for you to remain prepared for it.

When babies start to walk, they do not experiment too much during the initial stages and walk only within a familiar territory. It becomes important for you to safeguard these areas to ensure that they do not endanger themselves.

A staircase is still a place of danger as babies will not be able to control their movement. If they are using the walker then it is especially important to cordon off staircases.

Climbing is another aspect to beware of, as babies will want to climb on top of things in order to access something placed up high. This can be quite dangerous and will be important to ensure that such places are not accessible to your baby.

Toddlers will also be curious about electric points so make sure you block all of them in areas where the child is likely to be playing. Your baby will start to learn the importance of safety as and when he/she gets older but until such time you have to take measures to safeguard the child.

These form the two main aspects of preparation for the time your baby starts to crawl until he/she learns to walk independently. Remember, a child who is standing up sees more and is liable to grab for things. Thus, keep things within his/her reach level at a minimum.

Sleep training

It is obvious that parents will want their children to get accustomed to sleeping alone in their own rooms. For this, parents will have to train their children to sleep in their own beds. Here is a guide to follow.

- Set up a comfortable room for your toddler. Place their toys and favorite blanket into that room, so that they feel like returning to their bed every night. Keep a night light on when they sleep, as they will be able to sleep better.

- Place photos of yourself in the room so that they can see you. It will also help them sleep better.

- You have the choice to make use of the Ferber method where you allow the child to cry for a certain time before receiving external comfort. Although this might seem like a cruel activity, it's been proven to be helpful in training children to sleep alone after a week or so.

- Read them a bedtime story so that they fall asleep. Some light music before sleep also helps in soothing them and putting them to sleep.

Chapter 4: Spending Prime Time Together

Fathers and children need time together, but a father also needs perhaps to go out to work. If you can't attend school functions, explain to your kids about it in advance and they won't be too disheartened. Fathers tend to leave it a bit too late to apologize because they dread the child's reaction. The child reacts in a much more understanding way if the child is told the reasons. I remember an important sports event that my father could not attend. I was hurt. I was proud of my achievements and wanted to share them with him. However, we found a new solution and you can too. If you can't be there, make sure someone is who can photograph the important parts of the event. That way you show the kids that you really do care and when you have time, after work, you can spend some prime time enjoying their achievements with them, even though you could not be at the event.

The time that you do spend together should always be prime time. Even sitting at the breakfast table together gives you a chance to talk to your kids and see how they are doing. A man may have to organize family life in a different way to a woman, but it's always going to be important that he remembers all of the events that make up a child's life and that he is prepared for things that can happen:

- Child illness
- Kid's homework
- Spending family time watching a movie
- Taking pets out for walks together
- Teaching kids to be self-sufficient

The path of childhood even with two parents isn't clear-cut. Things can happen that throw a spanner into the works and it isn't just single fathers who suffer from the unpredictable nature of child rearing. Don't apologize for your lack of expertise. Instead, make the children aware that you are always there for them but that sometimes, it takes a bit of working out to fit all their schedules into everyday life.

The main thing to remember is that the relationship between children and their father should be based on trust. Your need to cater for their welfare must go hand in hand with kids seeing that you care. If you make mistakes along the way, don't make the kids feel like they are getting in your way. That's a pretty awful response to something happening. I remember getting measles and becoming a difficulty for my own dad. The way he dealt with it was very good because he didn't make me feel like I was a nuisance. Instead, he rang work to say he had something to deal with and found someone to stay with me during the day while he was gone. There was no begrudging anger and I wasn't made to feel that I was getting in the way of his life and that's vital to the equation.

The thing that you will have to get used to as a parent is that children bring a certain about of unpredictability to your life. You need to be open to changes and you also need to be extremely positive to the point of exhaustion sometimes, but you never need to feel guilty because you can't be there all of the time. It's not practical that you are and the children do need to see the true perspective, but you can make allowances for those times you are not there with a little thought.

"I can't be at the school concert because I have overtime to do," doesn't sound like a really good excuse to a child. "I wish I could be there baby. Perhaps your brother can video it for me so I get to see you in that gorgeous dress," is a better response. There's no explanation needed and you are showing the child that it's your wish to see them but that life is getting in the way and making you sad because you can't.

If you spend more time with your kids whenever you can, you learn what makes them tick and you can make it a very positive experience. Reading them a goodnight story or listening to them recite a poem they wrote are all part and parcel of enjoying your kids and even if you are a little tired, it doesn't hurt to let them spend a little time with you to talk about the things that are important to them.

Think of it as an exercise in getting to know the characters of your kids because when you do, that makes things a whole lot easier. When my dad discovered I liked music, he didn't always have to be there. He provided me with great music to listen to and by doing so, showed an interest in my interest. My brother, on the other hand, was more interested in sports and we made sure among the family that dad was able to enjoy a few baskets in the evening with him, so that they got a chance to have a father son moment together as this helped considerably with taking strain out of the relationship between them following the divorce.

Prime time involves laughing with your kids and showing them that you used to be a kid too. It means letting them know you're not perfect and being able to laugh at your own mistakes. My father dyed my school shirt pink because he didn't know how to split the washing into colored and white, but we laughed about it and he learned. All of the dilemmas of today will pass and build up into family memories. If you offer your kids a secure home, lots of love and attention and show them you make mistakes too, this builds the bond between you on an equal basis and helps you to learn to be a great dad.

Chapter 5: Parenting Pitfalls

1. A child who is secretive and finds it difficult to trust people is so, because her parents are irritable and easily lose their calm. This leads the child into believing that anything that she says or does will lead to an extreme reaction by her parents. So she chooses to be secretive.

2. A child who is shy and extremely indecisive is a result of parents' protective behaviour. Making decisions for her, not letting her do small tasks on her own, and not letting her grow leads to lack of confidence in the child.

3. A child who is constantly eyeing other children's belongings and is easily amused by things she doesn't own, is because the

parents deny her the right to choose. It is not enough to provide a child with what the parents believe is right for her, it is equally important to take into consideration the child's liking.

4.A child who gets jealous of others and shows signs of envy, is prey to a lot of comparison by her parents. Parents who are constantly comparing their child to others are setting their child up for a life of constant insecurity.

5.A child who gets jealous of others and shows signs of envy, is prey to a lot of comparison by her parents. Parents who are constantly comparing their child to others are setting their child up for a life of constant insecurity.

6.A child who is rude to the others around her, is following an example set by her parents or another close family member.

7.A child who is irritable and shows bad temper, is so, due to the lack of attention she gets. Parents who don't make time for their child and simply don't pay heed to what the child has to say, lead the child into believing that throwing a tantrum or showing extreme behaviour is the only way she will get noticed.

8.A child who lies to her parents, is probably doing so because telling the truth in the past must have led her parents to react negatively. This kind of behaviour makes the child believe that hiding the truth will keep her in her parents' good books.

9.A child who doesn't respect others and their feelings is a result of parents not acknowledging her feelings. Parents who expect their child to follow what they tell her, without considering her outlook or emotions, lead her into believing that it is okay to not respect others.

10.A child who is too nervous to take a stand in a situation or stand up for herself, is scarred by incidents of when her parents berated her in front of others.

Successful Parenting: Evolving Is The Key, Not Making Another True Copy Of Oneself

The success of parenting cannot be measured by what and how much a parent can do for their child. It depends on how capable the parent has made their child, to do things for herself that will lead to her success.

As an individual, every parent is the product of their upbringing and their experience with the world around them. The manner in which a person thinks, reacts and decides what is right and wrong, is built on their individual understanding of things, and sometimes it's purely based on blind faith and unquestioned beliefs that have been transferred to them from generation to generation, their culture and the society of which they are a part of.

The idea is to get rid of anything that does not make sense or align with one's understanding of things. This is so important because, when parents tell their child to do a certain thing because they believe it is right, or when they ask her in believe something because that's how everyone has been doing it for years, the child will more often than not, at some point, question the logic or science behind it. In such cases, if parents themselves don't understand the very essence of why they do or believe in certain things, it is unfair to expect their children to be blind followers of the same.

Chapter 6: Disciplining Your Child

Parenting is a tough job. Raising kids is all giving them what they need, some of what they want, and most of all, implementing discipline. The word **discipline** brings with it a string of negative connotations. Loud arguments, headaches, and a lot of spanking are usually what come to mind when people talk about disciplining a child. Teaching discipline to your child is most probably the hardest part about being a parent.

Discipline is basically a form of conditioning wherein certain behaviors are either reinforced or discouraged, using rewards and punishments. A child is taught to follow a standard of behavior. Discipline starts within the family and parents are the foremost people responsible for disciplining a child.

Discipline is basically of two types: the traditional way and the new method called positive discipline. The traditional method of discipline involves spanking and scolding. The parent is seen as the absolute authority. The child is completely controlled by the parents. They are required to act according to how the parents regard as right and wrong behavior. Spanking has been a time-honored way of disciplining children. It aims to instill fear in the child as a way of keeping them in line.

Child psychologists and child care experts caution against the traditional way of correcting misbehaving kids though. Shame and humiliation result from it and serve no other purpose. It creates behavioral and emotional problems that may persist until the child becomes an adult. The bond between the parent and the child, no matter how healthy it may be, becomes damaged. The message it gives to children is that violence is the only effective solution to problems.

Children who are disciplined the traditional way are more aggressive towards other children. When they become teenagers, they are more likely to rebel against their parents. Instead of thinking how to control themselves and behave better, children who are punished harshly think more about self-justification and revenge. The motivation is more on how to avoid punishment rather than how to change the negative behavior. Deception and telling lies become more prevalent in order to avoid punishment.

Several studies have shown that children develop problems in different aspects of their lives, which persist until adulthood. The emotional bond they have with their parents become negatively affected. They rebel and harbor ill feelings towards their parents. Instead of looking up to their parents as role models, they do the exact opposite.These problems and conflicts also affect how they are as parents later on. They unconsciously become like their parents. These issues transcend several generations.

Fear, control and manipulation that come with traditional discipline are linked to several adult problems. Children grow up having problems with forming social and emotional relationships. They defy authority in the society. Fear instilled in children may later influence them to lead a life of crime.On a personal level, they have difficulty forming healthy relationships. They are less attached to their partners, and less committing to the relationship. They are also prone to be an abuser or be the abused. Getting spanked as a child sends them a message that physical force can make things right. You can hurt people you love when you see it as appropriate for them. That it is OK to be physically and verbally hurt by people you love. These are all wrong messages given to children growing up with spanking.

Most experts recommend a gentler approach towards disciplining children. Beginning at birth, parents are encouraged to form strong attachment and develop trust with their infant. This is achieved through consistent and loving response to the infant's needs. These bonds become the foundation of discipline later on as the child grows older. A healthy and strong parent-child relationship is the best foundation to discipline a child.

Chapter 7

In an ideal world, spanking would never be needed. However, on rare occasions it may be necessary to smack your child's bottom. This book does not intend to either promote or discourage the practice, but rather give parents accurate instruction on using infrequent non-abusive spanking as a discipline.

Spanking is a much-debated topic. Most child behavior professionals do not recommend any form of corporal punishment as a discipline method for children. However, a few trained experts and many parents will tell you that a spanking given with fairness, love and care is an effective way to reverse dreadful bad behavior. The decision as to the usefulness of spanking is best made by a child's parent.

It is unfortunate that there are many kids who are abused under the pretext of spanking, and this book is an attempt to inform parents in a way that would prevent mistreatment. The following information offers alternatives and suggests when, where, and how spanking should be handled.

This accounting absolutely condemns the practice when associated with a quick-fix solution without understanding the consequences of the action. In addition to giving personal examples and setting clear guidelines with standards for your children and reinforcing positive behavior, always ask yourself if the extreme alternative is absolutely necessary. Should You Spank Your Child?

Were you ever spanked? Then you may think it's a good way to influence a child. Or maybe you don't want to spank, but you find yourself doing it because you don't know how else to get their attention and that their behavior is totally unacceptable. Interestingly, adults who were not spanked as children don't generally spank their kids. It just feels wrong to them. They find other ways to get through and they claim their children turn out fine. In fact, they truly believe that many of the kids who are spanked might have a harder time regulating their emotions, and frequently get into more trouble.

So if you were spanked and think you came out alright, it may possibly be because of the spanking. On the other hand, you might believe you'd be better off if not spanked.

Chapter 8: What Is The Terrible Twos?

You have probably experienced this; your toddler as the natural beautiful little angel is looking at you with his big and cute eyes, you know, like those precious moments cartoons and figurines you've seen out there. So innocent, so cuddly and with a full smile that just melts the heck out of you. Then all of a sudden something happens, your little angel totally changes into what almost appears to be a possessed child, sometimes you may get a vague idea of what triggered it but sometimes you just have no idea at all! It escalates from yelling to screaming and kicking with rage. Oh dear lord not again!

Yup, the terrible twos is here! Most parents have experienced this and it can be extremely frustrating not knowing what to do or how to handle it. Heck, some parents even go through this all the way into the threes and even fours! It can be hard to see your adorable child so happy one day and so out of control and even scary the next.

There are a few ways to deal with your child that is going through the terrible twos, but the main thing is to understand why, if you don't then you won't know why something you tried didn't work. One important thing to mention as well is that consistency is another key, even if you learn more than a couple strategies you can use, you should do it in a consistent way to give it a chance to make it work; this way you will find out one of the strategies and tips you will learn will work fine if not at least minimize the outbursts.It also makes a tremendous difference the way the you and family members around your child react, by losing control and becoming angry for example; it is more likely to make it worstfor your toddler and for yourself.

The main thing to understandis that the terrible twos is a common developmental stage that your child goes through, and usually starts about at the age of two; hence the name "the terrible twos", but sometimes as early as 18 months, and they can last up until age 4. It is very important for you as the parent to know and understand that your toddler is not trying to be rebellious because he wants to; but simply growing up, starting to realize he is capable of doing things for himself and just becomes frustrated when he can't communicate or express his needs through the language that we as older and more mature adults know.

Having that very simple understanding on what the terrible twos is essential. It will be important for you to know what to do in different situations as depending on that, you will have to act a little differently to get the best results. Just remember to always keep your cool and ignore the temper tantrum itself as what you will need to tackle is not that per say but making the child understand that you understand his frustration and are there for him. Never yell back at a child for that will only make things worse as you will now have two frustrated people instead of one. Speaking in a calm or normal tone is always best as you are also teaching your child that it is best to solve problems this way, especially at their early age when they are like sponges absorbing everything the experience in their surroundings.

When Your Child Bites And Hits

Sometimes when your toddler is in his terrible twos, you will find out that he bites and even hits you or other little kids! There is a lot of controversy between some parents suggesting that lightly hitting your toddler back or spanking him after he hits or bites so that he knows how it feels is an effective way to teach the child about what he is doing when it comes to biting or hitting.

In a way yes, it may be a way for you to let your child know how it feels because this way he will learn from first person experience that it does actually hurt to be bitten, or hit by other people. But in my experience as a mom, and having taken care of other toddlers, in the long run this seems to teach young children that this is an acceptable form of venting, in essence even if you apply what some call "harmless violence" such as letting your toddler hit a pillow is still teaching them that hitting is an acceptable form of solving the feeling of anger.

After doing some research and trying a few things of my own I learned that the best way was to completely ignore him. Yes this may sound a bit ridicule at first but let me tell you, this was an effective method I used whenever he bit or hit me and it worked! The only thing with doing this is that it does take time since you may have to do it several times before your child gets it. Basically what is happening here is that your child is trying to get your reaction and if you give in or have the reaction he is looking for as he hits or bites you, you will have created an "anchor" that is stored in his little mind of his that this is the reaction he was looking for so he will simply keep on doing it! So simply walk away from the situation or do something different, and try to do it without doing any facial expressions as your toddler will see this as well, quietly move away without saying a word. By ignoring him for completely, he will notice that you simply don't react to his biting and hitting and as you keep on doing this whenever he does it, he will then stop doing it.

If your child is a little older and hitting other children or people, then he is capable of understanding a little better now between right and wrong. As I noted earlier, I am not a fan of physically disciplining children going in their terrible twos. So here's what I recommend: When your toddler hits another person, grab her and move away from the scene, make sure you firmly look into his eyes and by mentioning his name tell him "no biting" or "no hitting", "biting hurts people, we do not do that". It is really important to use a firm voice when doing this, and by also having your child look at you in the eyes you will also communicate that you really mean it.

Remember that we are not trying to correct the fact that the child is acting angry, because anger is a natural feeling we all go through, but the expression of behaving in a violent manner. Going back to what we mentioned earlier, many of the children's behaviors are due to frustration of being unable to communicate how they feel, and by being able to communicate to them that we understand that they are feeling angry, we are acknowledging their feeling. At the same time you are teaching your young little one that using our words is far more constructive rather than solving things through violence. Let him know that he can use his words to express he is angry and that he can talk to you about it.

When it comes to biting, it doesn't mean that you are a bad parent teaching your toddler violence, they simply do it because they are unable to express their emotions through words, they are still very young and this is normal. Setting rules helps. Just as other forms of discipline, we need to teach children rules. Children need discipline but most importantly above everything else, we need to show them love and caregiving as these are at the same time ways to show them that we really do care and are there for them, this is the most important thing to remember, now going back to setting rules and boundaries we are also giving them the tools by which to abide from. Certainly, biting is against the rules and you should make that clear in advance.

One of the best ways to help this situation in the long run is by carefully observing your toddler, as many young children are just frustrated about something and they do not have a better way of expressing it.

You will find signs of what is frustrating it, and therefore be able to do something to improve that area.

For example, it could be as simple as not having taught him how to use his words to express anger, or perhaps he feels that no one is listening to him or is even feeling attacked by other children. Paying attention to what triggers it is a great way to decipher where the frustration is coming from and making the necessary changes or taking the necessary action to correct it to minimize or eliminate the problem.

Chapter 9: What Is Parenting All About?

Parenting is God's honour given to humanity for administering His laws, principles and precepts in moulding this new life you "brought" into this world. Donating your twenty-three set of chromosomes does not make you a parent; however, it does qualify you to be one. Beyond the biological interaction between two parties in the conception of a child, there exists a world entirely independent of biological relations or connection. Those who have adopted children clearly demonstrate and better emphasize this point to the fullest.

The biological connection between a child and its parent is a delivery vehicle that carries all sorts of genetic links which gives him his predecessors' diverse dispositions; and these usually help to "confirm" your positional-claim among your kin folk. Parenting on the other hand could or could not have any biological connection between the parent and a child. Therefore, fathering children and parenting them are two different roles a man can fulfil by choice or default. A father (or mother) can be both a father and a parent but a parent on the other hand might not have any biological connection to a child.

In some cases, even siblings fulfil the parental role to the best description possible. God indeed made man perfect in all respects but man simply sought out ways and means to corrupt that perfection. Had it not been for man's schemes and what not, we would not be where we are today, where children are confused as to who their parents are between those of genetic descent and those who fulfilled parental roles in their lives.

In some cultures, it is said that it takes a village to raise a child while other cultures emphasizes the "rule" of keeping one's child as far away from strangers as possible. The former pay their respects to strangers in a ways that would make you embrace the concept of being a stranger. They purchase special items for "visitors" (where the word visitor caries a dual meaning, namely: someone who visits you from far out of your locality irrespective of your relation with him or her; it is also used in reference to those who visit as regular visitors, your acquaintances, friends and relatives) to be used when by some chance they come your way. These items range from kitchenware, bedding (including bedrooms) and sometimes even fattened animals and fowls make it to this list.

I would say it is only fair for such a person (visitor/stranger) to return the favour bestowed to him by playing the parental role to my child at an hour when my child needs guidance or protection especially in my absence.

Fulfilment in human life comes in various forms and wrappings of both glitter and non-glitter packages. Giving guidance to a child even if it is for but a moment is one of those fulfilling "duties" of human life. When one withholds a good thing due to a child at an hour of the child's need when he (parent/adult) is the only one available and it is in his power to meet the child's need and he decides not to; that person at that hour is devoid of humanity. In general, human beings reach a stage in their lives where their God-given instincts kick-in and all they ever want to do is play a parental role in a child's life. When this time comes, all myths about marriage and family life simply evaporates into nothingness. Friends are left amazed and perplexed about this new development, which seemingly came overnight to do no small damage in "our-well-principled-fan-club".

When this sense of duty calls, friends lose friends, non-committing-partners lose committing-partners and siblings lose siblings. Look at the faces of those who gain, their naïve and innocent smiles speak volumes about their gains. Those chubby cheeks become victims of loving-kisses and gentle-strokes from the hands of caring parent-filled-hearts. Caring for someone who is vulnerable to your love and tender-care is beyond comparison.

Children look up to their parents to "fill-in" the missing things in their lives, the magnitude of this expectation by a child is the one that sometimes drive parents to do and say unimaginable things. In an attempt to drive a lesson home about heroic acts of manhood it is very easy to find men and women relate stories of how a hero single-handedly saved a helpless victim from the hands of a merciless monster whose intention was to completely annihilate the poor victim. To add a rather "sweeter" taste to the mix, the poor victim has to be a woman. These stories and the like form a great part of negative parenting from both men and women. If the merciless monster is likened to Mr XYZ, then we are painting not only a distorted picture for our children, but we are also labelling all Mr XYZ look-alikes as the same merciless monsters to the children's minds and from such pictures stereo-types and prejudices are born.

Chapter 10: Being A Single Parent Does Not Mean Raising An Unstable Child

Teamwork is essential when it comes to the task of raising children. Said teamwork is made much easier when the two parents are together and living under the same roof, as each can take turns with the responsibilities that go along with child-rearing while giving the other a chance to take a short break in the interim.

On the other hand, there is that group of single parents who do not have the luxury of relying on one another when it comes to the grind of daily life with the children. As the divorce rate continues its upward climb, single parent families are seemingly becoming the norm.

As a matter of fact, single parenting statistics cite that approximately 13.6 million adults in the United States are presently raising their minor children in the one-parent environment. In many instances the occurrence of raising a child as a single parent is the outcome of a divorce in the family. As a result, the number of single father parenting households is on the rise.

Yet no matter how prevalent the situation of being a single parent has become, there are still several parenting myths that go along with the notion of bringing up a child by oneself. First on the single parenting myth list is the idea that the mother will be rewarded with the custody of a child a majority of the time.

Though this notion might have been true ten or more years ago, much has changed in the field of family law since that time period. As long as both parents are mentally and physically healthy and stable, a judge will make a custodial decision based on the following factors:

☐ The amount of income each parent brings in

☐The safety of the residential area where each parent has made his or her home

- The quality of the school districts in said areas
- Other miscellaneous aspects that will aid the judge in making the right decision on behalf of the minor children.

Therefore, if it is the father who meets the above criteria more successfully than the mother, it should be expected that he is awarded primary custody of the couple's youngsters.

Next on the single parenting myth list is the belief that children in single parent homes have more behavioral problems than those adolescents who live with both their mother and their father. It is true that the best scenario for any child enmeshed in the stages of growing up is to have his or her two parents present in the same household. But if a child is being raised in a single parent atmosphere, this situation does not automatically turn that child into a disciplinary challenge.

In other words, youngsters brought up by single parents are no more likely to abuse drugs or alcohol or receive bad grades in school than their peers living in homes where the parents are married, as many studies have shown.

The third myth regarding single parenting is the suggestion that a single parenting home is also a broken home. Many spouses who have chosen to divorce have cited this decision as the reason why their homes are no longer considered "broken" because after the divorce is final, the two warring parents are no longer situated under the same roof and consequently exposing their children to the perpetual fights between the adults.

It is not true that children in single parent families have lower self-esteem than those adolescents living with both of their parents. Thus, this incorrect belief comprises the next single parenting myth. One of the main factors that affects the self-esteem of children is the income level of their parents.

For example, it is quite difficult for a child to watch as his friends receive all the hot toys on the market during the winter holidays, but because his parents (single or married) are in the bracket of lower earning he knows he won't see any of those toys for himself.

And since a two-parent family can be just as likely to experience income issues as a single parent family, the children from a single parent household are no more or less susceptible to self-esteem problems than those from a family of two parents.

The fifth and final myth on the single parenting subject has to do with child support payments from one spouse to the other.

The amount of child support paid is based in part on the number of days of the year the paying parent spends with the minor children. If the two parents decide they want to share equal custody and therefore equal time with their children, the paid child support total will decrease as a result.

Does this mean the children suffer because the parent receiving the payments now has less money to spend when they are in her custodial care?

The answer to this question is also what debunks the myth. Child support payments are doled out to compensate for the time the paying parent is not spending with the minor children.

To put it another way, if one parent has primary custody then he or she naturally spends more funds on the children, which is where the child support comes in to help cover that additional money spent.

But money cannot replace the time spent with a parent, which is why a child is better off having equal time with each adult in place of the payments his other parent would receive instead. It is common knowledge that the ideal situation for children is to live with both parents.

Regardless, it is comforting to know that if a child must be brought up in a single parent home, he has just as much a chance of successfully thriving in his future life as a child who has both of his parents together on a daily basis.

Chapter 11: The Parent Game

Nothing you do for children is ever wasted. They seem not to notice us, hovering, averting our eyes, and they seldom offer thanks, but what we do for them is never wasted.

Garrison Keillor

All children are beautiful. Their purity and absence of guile makes them so. They are at the same time unique and yet marked with the evidence of our parenthood. Not only in looks or mannerisms, but also in the sense that they grow up to reflect all that you have invested as a parent.

A child will adopt your values and goals; the way that you interact with the world and everyone in it. They learn how to deal with life, from you.

For some, the challenge of winning the parenting game comes with preparation. For others it is an unintended result. For yet others it is the culmination of a happily anticipated goal.

Whatever brings you to the role, parenting is not a game in the sense that it is not a pastime or an activity to while away the hours. It is an investment in the future—yours, theirs and ours.

This makes it a responsibility that we need to take seriously, although humor often makes the difference between a lesson learned and a punishment rendered. It's a test of our most human tendencies. Can we…

be wise when experience and wisdom is the only solution to a problem?

be patient when they make mistakes and struggle to find their way in the world?

be resourceful when their needs exceed what is readily at hand?

be a child when it's time to play and an adult when it's not?

be strong when they falter without smothering their need to find their own way?

be loyal to each as individuals and to the whole at the same time?

be loving in the face of their rebellion?

be the best we know how to be, even when life has us down?

Make no mistake; parenting is not an easy job. Yet it is one we take on willingly. When we discover we are to become a parent there is that very normal moment when we are filled with doubt. What have I done? How will my life change? Can I really take care of another life beside my own?

The answer, of course, is yes. There is no secret recipe. We each have, within ourselves, the ability to be the best parent imaginable.We can not only play, but win, the parenting game.

Let's get started!

Chapter 12: Categorise

Take your list from Activity 2 and split each item into one of three categories:

Quick-fix

Temporary or circumstantial

Life-altering

Coping on the Hard Days

Great. We've acknowledged that we are suffering. We've identified why we're suffering and we've broken our suffering down into categories. So from here on out it's plain sailing, right? Sadly, no.

Now the hard work starts.

Some days are okay. We feel positive. We feel hopeful. We know that the sun will shine again and the moon will rise again and the seasons will change and life will go on.

Other days we can't breathe through the pain, the anxiety, and the uncertainty. And yet, on those days we still have to parent. We still have to feed and clothe and play and ferry and cajole and entertain or educate or at least be near our children. Those are the hardest days of parenting. Very few of us actually have the opportunity to Eat, Pray, Love our way around the world while we sort through our heartache.

After my mother died, and everyone was around, needing me, I was fine. When everyone went home, I went to bed totally okay, and couldn't get out of it again for almost 7 days. And yet on those days, my children still needed their mother.

I don't think there's anything in this world harder than being a parent – being a good parent – on the days where you just want to give up.

In my experience over four variably dark years (remember, I said it ranged from 'hard' to 'I don't want to be here anymore') there are ways of coping. Not each way will work for every person or every situation. Start with the ones that resonate with you. And on the next extremely tough day, try them. Even try the ones you don't feel like trying.

Choose to cope

I can give you every coping technique in the world, print it on your walls, paint it on your ceilings, but every day you have to choose to want to cope. I know that walking around with a thundercloud over your head can feel almost comforting.

There's a solemn satisfaction in drowning in your own misery, but it's those days that the children are on their worst behaviour. You know that it's probably you as much as them, but in that moment, it's so much easier to blame them.

If you want to improve things, and have a happier home, despite your sorrow/anxiety/anger/pain/suffering you have to choose to cope.

Activity 4: Choose to cope

Write a short note to yourself with at least three reasons why you think you should choose to cope? What would be your reward, if you could make it through today?

As A Man Thinketh

James Allen in his 1903 book As A Man Thinketh writes,

"As he thinks, so he is; as he continues to think, so he remains."

This used to anger me so much. I'm heartbroken! That's why I'm sad, that's why I don't want to make you dinner, that's why I can't face doing the laundry! And no, I don't care about your stupid dolly's song, I'm in pain here, PAIN!

Heartbreak might be a fact. But you don't have to be a victim to it. You don't have to let it eat you alive. And I say this knowing full well how at times, I have allowed it to consume me.

But you can choose to live through your heartbreak, through your pain, through your financial strain. You can choose to not harm your relationships, to not wound your children. You don't have to want to do it. You just have to do it.

How can you change your mindset when you're drowning in the overwhelm of emotion?

Get Active

Go for a walk

Stand outside and take deep (sometimes painful as you fight back the urge to scream) breaths

Lie on your bed and scream into your pillow

Sit out in the sun for a few minutes. Close your eyes and really feel the sun on your skin

Do something you think you simply don't have the time to do

Laugh. Sit on the ground facing your child and laugh. They will think you've lost your mind, and they will start laughing, and their laughter will be contagious

Ask your children if you can join their game (I find this one almost impossibly hard when my head isn't in the right place, but it can work!)

Be popcorn. This means put on some music, make yourself into a small ball and unfurl, shouting pop as you jump up repeatedly. Get the kids to do it with you. They will be in hysterics, and you'll feel better.

You'll feel better?

Momentarily. Yes. You'll flood your body with endorphins, the feel-good hormones, and you will lighten the thundercloud over your head. This will give you a boost, replenished you, or allow you to tackle one of those smaller things causing you frustration. Or you can simply 'be' without the pressure of your hardship choking you.

Chapter 13: Encouragement And Praise Make Your Child Feel Important

As good parents we need to give our kids encouragement and praise to make them feel important. We need to help them define and work towards specific goals. The biggest mistake we can make is to tell them that winning and results are all that matter versus the effort they make to accomplish their goals.

Some parents have the tendency to pamper or spoil their kids. They do things for their child that they can and should do on their own. They pick up their room for them, wake them up in the morning or make their lunch. It is better to encourage and praise them for taking the responsibility of doing these things for themselves that will help them be less dependent on others.

It should be noted that encouragement and praise are not the same thing. Praise should be given for outstanding achievement. It can also promote some level of competition with fear of failure. Encouragement inspires self-esteem, improvement, effort, acceptance and confidence.

Even if they fail you should give them praise. Keep in mind that encouragement will not thrive on praise by itself. Make sure to be sincere in your praise as our kids can see through praise that is not real. There is always a risk with any child who is thirsty for praise will just try to float along in life and won't feel okay without praise. When you give encouragement focus on their assets and strengths and not their faults. Accept them as they are and at whatever level of accomplishment they are at.

Expectations that are unrealistic can be stressful for our kids. If there are conditions or some sort of physical restriction that prevents your child from completing some of the expectations, do not make the mistake of giving them false hope by saying they can do it. It's like taking them to the doctor for a shot and telling them it won't hurt. Eliminate their frustration with honesty and truth. Keep their trust intact instead of hoping that you can somehow fool them.

There are times when you need to help your kids set achievable goals. If your child gets excited about wanting to enter a contest of some kind then cheer them on regardless what the contest is. Keep them from counting up what prizes they could win before they are even officially entered in the event. Make the process so much fun and explain what they are up against so that their effort of entering overshadows winning.

There are those that want to let permissiveness creep into their encouragement and praise for their child. By allowing this to happen it makes our kids not concerned about the rights of others. This happens when there is inconsistent discipline and can result in our child feeling that life isn't always fair. They experience a denial of their own feelings. Someone who is not related to their own feelings can not be related to others.

When we give encouragement or praise to make our kids feel important they will feel like they can give their opinions; be involved in decisions and show responsibility that is compatible within their capabilities.

When your kids reach the teenage years do not be expecting to change them. Instead be ready and willing to accept your own mistakes. Telling your teenage young adult that you are sorry will go a long way in removing the generation gap that has happened. Let them know that parents need encouragement and praise also.

Our kids develop positive behaviors when we praise them correctly. This can also shape and mold their future behavior. Some of the results of praising your child can be a feeling of positive feedback, higher self esteem, more confidence and pride. They will also be more confident in their abilities and feel they can do most anything. Your praise gives emphasis to the way they have acted, helps define who they are all as the result of the actions they have taken. If something your child does pleases you don't wait to let them know. Just their effort to do well should warrant praise even if the results are not perfect in the end. There is always something about our kids that warrant encouragement and praise.

We need to be alert to all behavior or actions that are worthy of sincere honest praise without going overboard. The best way to accomplish this is waiting for that good behavior that you previously missed but went without praising them and immediately give them praise. This will also help clarify for your child what behavior or actions are considered commendable. Make sure you are squarely looking into your childs eyes when you give them the praise to strengthen their actions of positive behavior. Showing them a warm smile or hugging them can also go a long way towards them understanding exactly what they have done to receive your praise.

You need to let your kids know exactly and state clearly what activities or behaviors you found praiseworthy. The worst thing you can do as a good parent is to follow encouragement or praise with any type of criticism. You must let them know what they did right, not what was wrong, and reward them.

Every day you need to let your kids know what a great person they are growing into by praising them for all their positive actions and behaviors. This daily encouragement and praise will truly make your child feel important.

Chapter 14: Proper Communication

Most teenagers often love it when their parents could openly communicate with them.Communication seems to be the number one cause why parents and children go their separate ways.If they don't have set standards for communication then most likely they would always end up arguing.Teenagers would love to argue especially if they know that they are right.As parents, they should set the rules of communication where it could be well understood.For example, they should both agree that while the one is explaining, the other party should be listening attentively without interrupting.Both parties should be given time to explain their sides.

Another thing: parents must always prioritize their children over other matters.So, when they know that their children need to say something important then they should hear them no matter how busy they are.Through proper communication, children could really feel that they are important.The trouble with this matter is when the children become too difficult to open up for a two-way communication, either they never listen or they never talk.If this happen, parents need to be more patient and lead the proper communication setup, this could be done through the following ways.

Parents should involve their children into a discussion by asking their views and opinions.If they never get a positive action from them, then they should never react too readily or too harshly but instead, give them hints that their views matter.When children feel that their opinions are of great importance, they for sure would be encouraged to share their thoughts and ideas.And when they did, for sure parents would be more proud on the ideas their children have.

Parents should not force their children to say something that they never want to share.By forcing them, children could even more shy out from them especially if they anticipate how they would react.Instead, give them more time to share it and if they do, never ever react negatively or harshly, or even laugh.Children whose parents are too critical on the things they say would no longer share whatever things to them.

By being models to their children, parents should always communicate in the house in such a jovial way possible.By having a good-humored conversation, children would be encouraged to speak and enjoy talking more and sharing with their parents.

In matters pertaining to problems, parents should be calmer in confronting their children.Once children see that their parents have more things to say which could be unfair for their side they would no longer explain more.For them, what could be the use of explaining if in the end they will still be judged as the bad guys?

and so, parents should be more careful in this kind of situation.

Parents should also avoid making quick and incomprehensible statements to their children.By doing so, children will be more confused and will never know how to react to what they say.Worst, they would think that parents think they are doing something wrong; they would be guilty and could react differently.

Chapter 15: Age Groups And Issues

The preceding chapter outlined the grief cycle that children go through in a divorce and this chapter will identify the typical behaviors and reactions that occur in children of different ages going through a divorce. Keep in mind that every child is different both emotionally and developmentally and not all children will react the same way. Children may be more emotionally or socially mature or immature than others in their age group and the information below is a general guideline only.

As a parent if you have any concerns about your child's behavior or emotional health going through a divorce, be sure to consult with your pediatrician to ensure there is not a medical issue; then ask for a referral to a child therapist or play therapist if there are no medical issues.

BIRTH TO FIVE YEARS

Often very young children between birth and five years of age initially seem to go through the divorce very easily and are accepting of the parenting schedules and changes. This may be largely due to the fact that they are not yet aware that this isn't the norm; however when they get a bit older they may start to display the grief cycle, even though the divorce happened many years ago.

Children at about the age of two are starting to develop a sense of trust and predictability in their world and their environment. When changes occur, often they feel like their world is out of control, leading to an increase in tantrums and emotional displays of frustration, anger and anxiety. Parents at this time need to keep routines between Mom's house and Dad's house as similar as possible, and both parents need to interact frequently with the child. Ideally the child should communicate with both parents every day either in person, by phone or even over webcams on the internet. The more that young children understand that they have a Mommy and a Daddy in their lives the more secure and loved they will feel, even at this young age.

Pictures of the child with both parents as well as a photograph album or other reminders of the relationship between both parents and the child are critical. It is especially important for the parent with the most parenting time, which is often the mother, to talk about the other parent frequently, reminding the child that both parents are working together providing security, love and attention. Young kids may also be shy or timid the first few times they spend time with the parent that has left the family home, so both parents have to be encouraging and supportive of this parenting time.

SIX TO EIGHT YEARS

In a lot of the divorce research and parenting information the six to eight year old kids are known as the "parent pleasers". They really do want Mom and Dad to feel good about themselves and to be emotionally happy and content in their new lives. These kids tend to want to talk about one parent to the other parent, and it is very critical to allow children to say positives and to feel good about the other parent in your home. Avoid sarcasm or questioning as this can cause the child to feel uncomfortable.

These kids also need to have their own feelings validated. Even though as the adult you may be relieved, thankful or even optimistic about the divorce, it is likely that the children at this age are sad and are feeling a sense of loneliness or helplessness during the divorce. Listening to them without judgment and allowing them to have their own feelings about the divorce and talking to you about them is critical. You may find that a counselor works best with this group of children as they may not really tell you what they feel because they think it will make you sad or upset. They can, however, talk to stranger that has no emotional stake in the conversation.

NINE TO TWELVE YEARS

The kids in the nine to twelve year old range tend to respond rather strongly to the divorce for many different reasons. One of the major issues is that they are struggling with their own identity - not quite children yet not quite teens either, so emotional changes hit this group particularly hard. It is not uncommon for children of this age to feel powerless, betrayed and rejected through divorce.

Nine to twelve year olds are also more aware that there may have been problems in the family, especially if they overheard some hostile or negative conversations between Mom and Dad. They may have already made up their mind that one parent is to blame for the divorce, which may make them feel that the "bad" parent needs to be punished by rejection. Often kids at this age decide they are not going to have any contact with the parent that they see as at fault for the divorce. Ultimately this actually harms the child as he or she needs to have both a mother and father in his or her life. Even the parent that has the child's full support must actively encourage and even facilitate the ongoing relationship between the child and the other parent. Typically once the child understands that Mom or Dad is still a good Mom or Dad they will be willing to engage with that parent, which only helps to maintain a loving relationship rather than resulting in a breakdown of that relationship.

THIRTEEN TO EIGHTEEN YEARS

Older children tend to respond to the divorce in two distinct ways. The first way is to see the divorce as something between the parents, and continue to have a good relationship with both. The second way is to see one parent as the victim and one as the villain, and simply refuse to interact with that parent. Again, it is very important to facilitate, encourage and even actively promote the interaction of the child with the parent, even if it is short or brief interactions.

Often the older children will volunteer to take on additional roles to help the family. It is critical that kids do not see themselves as responsible for the care and well being of the parents or siblings through the divorce. While they may volunteer to do a bit more, they should never feel obligated to become an adult in the household. It is critical for both parents to remember that these mature children are really just kids, and they need to have time for themselves.

Keep in mind that keeping the lines of communication open and spending time with your child each day discussing their accomplishments, concerns and questions can help both parents stay in touch with their children as well as address any concerns or problems the kids may be having. It is common for children to speak with one parent or the other, so parents must be able to communicate their children's concerns, interests and problems with each other so they can work together in a cohesive manner.

Chapter 16: Seven Ways To Spend Time With Your Kids

If you're having a hard time coming up with simple and fun activities that you can do with your kids, here are seven things you should definitely try doing with them:

Cooking – Try cooking your kids' favorite dinner with them. Be it some chocolate cupcakes or an Asian-style Pasta, make it a family activity everyone can enjoy. Involving them in something as simple as cooking food for the family shows how much you appreciate their efforts and trust them. Do this once or twice a week. Your kids will surely look forward to each meal that they cook with you. Plus, you can also use this time to talk about school, their hobbies or pretty much anything under the sun.

Shopping or Groceries – As much as you want to do your groceries without the hassle of bring your kids, this is actually an activity you can do as a family. It'll give you time to spend with them while doing an important chore. Talk about multi-tasking. It will also make you kids feel involved, needed and an important member of the family. You can also use this to teach your kid some management skills. Teach them how to get good bargains or saving money. Turn every shopping or grocery date into a life lesson that your kids will use and need in the future.

Stroll – Take the time to stroll with your kids around the neighborhood. You can take a walk at the park or ride a bicycle. Make this simple leisure activity a family moment. You can even suggest a race and the winner gets to skip doing the dishes. It may be simple but your kids will definitely have fun. Plus, kids like it when they can show to their friends and families that their parents have the time to spend with them.

Games – Surprise your kids with a fun game like treasure hunting inside the house or playing water gun. Have them suggest prizes or punishments. It doesn't have to be a grand prize. It can be as simple as getting to order their favorite pizza or watch their favorite TV show. Also grab this opportunity to teach your kids the importance of winning and how in life there are things you have to lose sometimes. You'll be surprised by how many moral lessons you can teach your kid from a simple game. It might not seem important now, but your kids will definitely need it in the future.

Camping – If you have the time, take your kids camping or fishing. This is a fun activity that you can make as a family tradition during summer or the holidays. It'll take you away from your job and let you focus on your kids for a couple of days. You'll be surprised with how many things you'll learn and hear from your kids. Build something together – Be it a scrapbook or a tree house, building something with your kid is something you should try do often. Working side by side will not only allow you to spend time with your kids but also show them how much you appreciate being involved in their lives. If your kids have a project in school, take a break from work and help them do their science project. If your kids want a tree house, help them build one. You can even make scrapbooks and photo albums together. Its might be a simple moment but it's something that your kids will look back to and cherish.

Tuck them in bed – You have no idea how important this is to kids. As much as possible, give them a hug or tuck them in bed at night. You'll get to steal a couple of minutes before they go to sleep and even have a chance to talk about personal things. These are simple moments that your kid will look back to when they're older. It's a simple gesture that kids want to experience. An act that says they are loved, cherished and safe. You can read them a story or tell them about yourself when you were their age.

There are plenty of ways to spend time with your kids and these are just some of it. Just be creative in coming up with activities that you can do together. Or, you can just wing it by grabbing a favorite snack, a couple of board games or watching your favorite TV show.

Just make sure that when you're spending time with your kids don't let anything distract you. Avoid talking about work or checking your email in front of them. If it's a family time, it's family time. That rule should apply not just on your kids but also on you.

Chapter 17: Step Dad Or Stepped On Dad

Stepdad, hmmm, does that mean that you are available to be stepped on or walked over?No, you are not a stepped on dad.You are an important part of your children's and step children's lives, even if they don't always respect you or your position as the dad in this house.

You will never be their stepkids' birth parent and you never will be.Even if the other parent is deceased the children may refer to him as "my real dad."That is okay. That is reality.But it is also reality that you are not necessarily worthless or inferior to the birth parent.You are each unique and provide different aspects to parenting.

Dad of This House

Most stepparents want more than respect. We hold the dream that we will also be loved and honored by them as we hope we can build a new family unit.Many therapists tell me that young children are very black and white and cannot deal in abstract thinking.

What this means is that when children begin to transfer affection to a step parent, they feel guilty and disloyal to the birth parent.They need to be told that it is okay to love many people and that it is good to have a number of adults who care and support them.

Don't Expect Instant Love

You may feel irritated or resentful of your stepchildren.You don't have to automatically love them, but you do have to act in a loving and respectful way towards them and their mother.

As you give and demand respect and kindness, you will create a shared life filled with memories. Love and affection take time to grow in any relationship.Many times, just looking at what the child might be feeling and having an honest and open communication will pave the road for a mutually respectful relationship.

Chapter 18: Making New Friends

There are times when your child will need to learn how to make new friends.These times include when they starting school or changing to a new school, if you move, or if people have moved into your neighborhood.This can be scary for some kids.Here are some ways to help your child make new friends.Give them something to do with the new friend.Asking another child to play in the sprinklers is less intimidating than just asking them to play.Your child will not have to worry about thinking of something to do when the friend comes over.Find instances when your child can talk to other children.When you go to the park, help your child say hi and be friendly to other kids.This will help them get over the shyness that can come when talking to someone they don't know. Make friends with the parents of new neighbors, and invite them and their children over.This can be less stressful for your kids and give them the confidence they need.You are close by, and they can watch you make new friends as well.Your example can teach them.Start out by having cousins come play if possible.If your child hasn't played with a lot of children, this can be an easy way to learn the social skills to get along with others.Family members are easier because you already know them, and they are less forgiving if your child decides to bite their child.Helping your child learn to make new friends is a great way to give them the confidence they need in school and throughout life.Using these tips and others can help make finding new friends easier.

Teaching kids about Holidays

We just finished the Fourth of July celebration at our house, and my five year old was told all about the parade and carnival, and fireworks to follow that evening.As we walked to the parade, he asked me why there were flags on a lot of the lawns.I realized that I didn't teach him about what the holiday meant. It doesn't matter what the holiday is, or what your beliefs are.If we don't teach our children what the holidays really mean, they are going to get a different idea than what we want. Often we get so caught up in preparing for the holidays that we don't spend the time that we should in teaching our children what the holiday means.

Before the holiday, take a half hour to spend teaching about the holiday.Give a brief overview of what the holiday is about, and find an activity that you can do with your children to reinforce their understanding.If you are teaching about Halloween, you can talk about the holiday before you carve pumpkins. We celebrate Christ's resurrection for Easter.One year I wanted to teach my children more about what Easter is really about.I found a recipe on the internet that makes a hollow cookie.Each ingredient symbolized something to do with the Easter holiday and Christ's resurrection.

My kids and I made the cookies and then put them in the oven overnight.When we woke up the next morning, the cookies were done, and they were hollow inside, representing an empty tomb. Whether you have a religious belief or just celebrate the commercial beliefs about holidays, there are meanings behind each holiday.Before we get caught up in the holiday itself, make sure your children understand that it is more than getting together with family, or dressing up in costumes.

The Independent Child

When my youngest child was just over one year old, I took him to run errands with a friend.As I was leaving the house, I put my son down and helped him walk down the stairs.As my friend watched from her car, she hollered out, "What are you doing, trying to make him grow up too fast?"I have thought about that a lot as I watch my son learn to do things for himself.I don't want him to grow up too fast but I want him to learn and develop.

Creating an independent child has a lot more to do with the parent than with the child.As a parent, we have to be able to let go and allow our children to try and fail.Sometimes this is too difficult for a parent, who will step in and assist.Unfortunately, our human nature often requires that we fail at something before we can learn how to succeed.When a mother or father steps in for the child, they are taking away that learning opportunity.

Start out small.

Teach your child something simple that they can try for themselves.Even children just learning to walk can be taught to do things for themselves.Give them a box to put toys in.Little kids love to put things in boxes.Show them how to clean up their toys, and give them a big smile and lots of praise when they do it.Two year olds can learn to make their beds.Resist the urge to go fix the bedspread when they are done.Let them do it themselves, and tell them how great they are when they do it. Creating independence is a lot about letting go of our own fears and having faith in our children.It's an important part of growing up, and one we shouldn't deny our children of learning.

Chapter 19: Financial Literacy. What Should You Teach Your Child?

Taboo.

It's been observed that in many families household finances are a taboo topic. Before you deny it, consider your own attitude. Many parents want to protect their children from inexorable market rules, therefore, they make their children believe that it's more honorable to give than to take. Materialism, as one of the business-related aspects, is also an undesirable trait in any society. And again, we moralize by teaching children that they shouldn't be motivated by profits. Instead of pursuing money or other material benefits, they should try to do good when they can.

And what do your family conversations look like? When children are too young, you answer their questions with vague comments, just to be left alone. And what happens when your children get older?

You're perfectly prepared to answer such questions as: "Where do babies come from?" or "Where did auntie Tracy go when she died?", but you feel overwhelmed by questions such as: "How much money does mommy get from her boss?" or "Why there's no money for vacation, but there is for a new car?".

Feeling uncomfortable when talking about finances with your children, may result from your own insufficient financial knowledge, or from being ashamed by small income and mishandling your finances. Or, it may be also caused by the fear that your child will share such private information with neighbor's children. However, it has consequences, as children grow up without any financial knowledge. They become adults with the knowledge of how to use a condom, but they don't know how to use a credit card. And this is their first step to find themselves on a slippery slope.

I'd like to present you a few most important lessons that you should teach your child.

Private property.

It sounds strange and too mature, doesn't it? And what would you say about a child who is to visit another child, and acts like a ruthless invader in other people's house? This child doesn't care about breaking a vase or destroying any other item in the house. Moreover, they claim another child's toys as their own. It resembles socialism a little bit, but actually, it's only the problem of a child who isn't familiar with the concept of private property.

How can you prevent it or change it? It's really simple. You need to repeat at every occasion what belongs to whom, no matter if it belongs to a child or an adult. When your child breaks an item, they should know the consequences: "You mustn't break anything, not because it's forbidden, but because it's a person's property, and every item has its value; if you break anything, you should replace it or fix it".

Children who don't understand the consequences of breaking someone's property, and who can have whatever they want by just pointing it in a store, are not aware of the concept of private property, or value of money.

Poverty and wealth.

Children learn about the world by observation, and sooner or later they notice the difference between the poor and the rich. You need to explain to them such issues as:

Some people have more money than others.

And there's nothing wrong with it. There is a limited amount of resources, and not everyone is rich, just like not everyone is poor.

- The more money you have, the more privileged you are.

Now let's forget about moral dilemmas for a moment. If a family can afford going to a concert, they go. If they can afford going on vacation abroad, they go. The same goes with having two cars, and a house at the seaside.When parents can afford expensive things, their child can see this. What those parents need to do, is to confirm their child's observation, and draw conclusions. If a person is better educated, or better predisposed, or simply works harder, they earn more money. And they can afford anything they want thanks to their skills, knowledge, and hard work.

Why is such a situation worth explaining to your child? Because if you don't do this, your child may unintentionally believe that rich people are thieves and fraudsters. And then your child has two options: either they'll always be poor or act immorally to become rich. Are there such people? Yes, there are. But you need to show your child another way to become affluent. There's nothing wrong in wanting to be rich. You just need to remember that you must work hard, wisely, and honestly.

- Money is earned, not given.

Money doesn't grow on trees. It seems obvious, but there are some complicated questions that may confuse any adult. You should explain to your child, that all money in the world is earned. If a person is given money because of some social benefits, it's because they earned it in the past, or someone else did, and donated to them. The best way of teaching your child how to get money, is by making them earn it on their own. Although your child can't have temporary job because they need to be at least 15 years old, there's always an uncle who needs help; your child may, for example, put labels on products in a factory, or pick up strawberries on a farm. The main idea is: If you want a skateboard, earn it.

The need of choice.

Your child may need to make a choice: should they spend their money on a bubblegum, or save it for a comic book? And that's when the issue of saving appears. You can read how to encourage your child to saving in the next chapters. But what's worth mentioning now, is that not only can you save money, but also invest them. How to teach your child investing? By having some entrepreneurial skills you can try the following (or similar) scheme: you give your child money which they save; they buy a sponge, a car wash product, and some other items required for your child's new business of washing cars.Calculate with your child how many cars they'd have to wash, and how much it would cost, so the investment pays off for itself. I can guarantee you, that after such an exercise (one is enough), your child will never miss the opportunity of making money.

Money is good. You can have it too.

Although the title of this paragraph may sound cliché, you can't deny that it's true. Children often receive contradictory messages. That's why you, as a parent and role model, should explain to your child that money isn't bad. If you have money, you don't have to worry if your family has a place to live, or anything to eat. Or if you can afford a dentist when you have a toothache. Moreover, if you have money, you can help others.

And what about possession? Don't foster the myth that the rich raise the rich, and the poor pass on their poverty to next generations. Teach your child, that life isn't about random social events. Let them know, that they aren't helpless when it comes to making choices, no matter where, and who they are; it doesn't matter if they're rich or poor, gifted or not, physically strong or weak. It's not the society who decides on your child's future or their income. It's your child themselves. And this is the most valuable lesson you can teach them. Young people should believe, that they're free to choose many things, and many paths. They should be aware that it's them who are responsible for their decisions.

To summarize.

Carefree living children may easily end up in an intellectually and morally inferior group. They may be surrounded by people susceptible to fads, moods, and political demagogy. By people, who are not confident about making important choices, and who lack self-reliance.

As a parent, who has an enormous influence on your child, think what you could possibly do to make your child understand the issues of goods trade, individual responsibility, the need of choice, and creating wealth. Maybe the information you give your child will be their first experience with the real economic world.

Chapter 20: Power Of Positive Parenting

Children should be disciplined so that the child can function well at home and in public. Every parent want their children to be happy, respectful and able to find their place in the world as well-behaved adults. Nobody wants to be accused of raising a spoiled brat.

Discipline is the process of teaching your child what type of behavior is acceptable and what type is not acceptable. It teaches a child to follow rules. It may involve both punishment, such as time-out, or rewards. Even though it sounds easy, every parent becomes frustrated at one time or another when it comes to discipline.

Your responsibility as a parent is to help your child become self-reliant, respectful and self-controlled. How is this done?

Reward good behavior:

Acknowledging good behavior is the best way to encourage your child to continue it.

Compliment your child when he or she shows the behavior you've been seeking.

Natural consequences:

If your child does something wrong, let him or her experience the result of that behavior. There is no need for you to lecture. Just make sure that the consequences they might experience are not dangerous.

Logical consequences:

It is similar to natural consequences but involves describing to your child what the consequences will be for unacceptable behavior. The consequence is directly linked to the behavior.

Taking away privileges:

Sometimes there is no logical or natural consequence for a bad behavior. Or you simply don't have time to think it through. So take away a privilege. This technique works best if the privilege is related some way to the behavior; if it is something the child values; or if it is taken away as soon as possible after the inappropriate behavior.

Time outs:

Time outs work if you know exactly what the child did wrong or if you need a break from the child's behavior. Be sure that you have a time-out location ahead of time. It should be a quiet, boring place. This method works best with younger kids for whom the separation from the parent is truly seen as a deprivation.

Discipline mistakes parents make

Sure, we all make mistakes. Even if we try to discipline our children. We must remember that our goal is not merely to get children to outwardly obey, but to reach their hearts with love. Here are a few pitfalls that we must guard against:

Bribing.

To bribe a child into obeying is to motivate him wrongly. Bribing encourages children in selfishness, as their motive for obeying is personal gain. Bribing sounds like, "If you clean your room you can rent a movie tonight" or "If you don't misbehave in the grocery store, you can pick out candy at the checkout counter." Children should be taught to obey because it is right. We should simply state the standard and follow through with consequences when that standard is violated.

Counting to Three.

We train our children to obey us. When we count to three, we cause our children to get into the habit of delayed obedience. Delayed obedience is disobedience. Counting to three encourages them to put off obeying until absolutely necessary. We want our children to view obedience as their best option, not a choice that is put off until the last minute.

Threatening.

This is one of the biggest struggles in parenting. We are often so tempted to say, "If you don't do this, then these will be the consequences." This is how we get ourselves in a pickle. If we tell them there will be a consequence then there better be one. Otherwise, we might cause them to question our word. A woman of integrity says what she means and means what she says. If we cry wolf too many times, we will eventually lose our effectiveness as well as the respect of our children. Our children need to have confidence that our word is our word.

Appealing to their emotions.

Parents often try to appeal to the emotions of the child by making them feel guilty. "After all I do for you, this is how you repay me," moans the parent with a sad face. It's easy for us to feel sorry for ourselves and think that our children "owe us" obedience. However, we want our children's motives for obeying to come from a heart to please - not from a parent inflicted guilt trip.

Reasoning with small children.

Parents should avoid trying to talk their children into obedience. Reasoning with small children erases the line of authority between the parent and the child, and places the parent in a position of being out smarted!We should avoid statements like, "Are you ready to go to bed?" and "Don't you think you should brush your teeth?" and "Why don't we pick up the toys before lunch?"

Asking the child if he would like to do something places him on a peer level with the parent.The parent who tries to reason with her child usually ends up frustrated, and the child usually ends up disrespecting her authority by arguing rather than obeying.

Repeating or going back on instructions.

In studying some the most of admirable and successful generals of our country, I have found that they all had one thing in common:they were certain of their commands before they issued them.Soldiers do not respect or respond well to an uncertain and inconsistent leader.

Chapter 21: Why We 'Never' Discipline Our Children

How ironic that we ended the last chapter with a scenario we have all seen in our local discount retailer.Allow me to take you to their parking lot for part two.It is a Saturday night and my family and I have had a long day out.We had promised our son that we would give him the opportunity to spend his allowance.So there we were- at Wally World.In the short trip between our last stop and the 'Made in China' bazaar, my son had hurt his baby sister, who is sitting next to him, not once, but twice.After the second offense I informed him that if **he chose** to hurt his sister again, **he also chose** not to spend his allowance that night.These statements were (are) repeated to make it abundantly clear what the consequence of the offense would be.

I pulled our minivan down a dark row of parking spaces.As I began to pull into the next closest space available, I heard a smack, followed by the shrill sound of my daughter crying.I did not say a word.I simply put the van in reverse and began to pull out of the parking lot.Noah started crying, knowing what this meant.He begged me to change my mind; that his behavior would now change.I calmly reminded him of our conversation and we drove home.

The title of this chapter is a simple argument of semantics.Do we do things in our house that you would quickly label as discipline?Absolutely!You caught us.However, you also did not.It is not the 'what' in our home that might seem foreign to you; it is the 'how.'For in all honesty, the 'how' was originally foreign to we two parents as well.But somewhere along the line, we were taught what I now give you the opportunity to learn.It can be said, with great certainty, that this simple semantic shift can very well reset the proper balance in a home.I say to you in complete confidence: this is the way that discipline was naturally intended to be balanced in the first place.

The most consistent law of the universe is that of cause and effect.'For every action there is an equal and opposite reaction.'Eastern Mystics call it Karma.Secularists say, 'what goes around, comes around.'Bible scholars say, 'you reap what you sow.'In fact, I would venture to guess that every religion in existence has a version of cause and effect in its core theology.

We do not punish (which is a cause) our children (who are effected).We allow our children to experience the consequences (which is an effect) of their own actions (which is the cause).This may be the most important semantic argument to the parenting process as a whole.I was raised in a family where if you did not do what you were told to do, then mom and dad would punish you (note: **mom** and **dad punish)**.Mom and Dad are the subject.Punish is the predicate.The child is a modifier when said child should be the subject of this sentence.

However, a consequence is the result (the effect) of the action taken.No longer is the focus on how mom and dad choose to respond.In fact, the choice has been made for them.The consequence was predetermined as the effect of the cause (i.e., jump off a cliff and gravity will suck you toward Terra Firma).The child knows before the offense is committed what the resulting effect will be.Imagine, being able to look your child in the face as they tear up about the pending consequence, and say, 'you knew when you chose to do what you did, what the consequence would be.Therefore, you **chose** the consequence.' For example, if the consequence of predetermined action was the forfeiting of a cell phone for a week, you- the parent- are not taking the phone away. She- the child- chose to forfeit the phone. Do you see the shift in the relationship of protagonist/antagonist? You- the parent- are no longer the 'bad guy.'

And honestly, that is the way it should be. All of us roll our eyes when a criminal tries to say that the police professionals are the problem. Police professionals are not perfect. But typically, those who do not violate a system of laws that all have predetermined consequences do not end up in a position where they need to 'spin' the situation and blame their consequences on someone else's actions. Parents are no different. We are not the 'bad guys.' Darth Vader may have been Luke's father, but most of us do not give in to the 'dark side.' We are simply trying to do the best we can to give our children half a chance in this crazy, mixed up world.

But often times the emotions surrounding discipline leave us drained.We raise our voices.We are tired from the rest of our day.We would much rather spend what time we do have with our children in a more positive frame of mind.But, there in, lies the simplicity of the need.Our children need to face the consequences of their own actions as much as we do.In doing so, we prepare them for life.Instead of believing that they are lorded over, 'consequence framing' lets your children make their own decisions, knowing that if they make the wrong one, they choose to face the predetermined consequence.

But in this discussion let us not forget that what our children need most is the 'consequences' of positive actions.Children need to know that the best way to get the love and attention they desire from you is to be the best he or she he or she can be.Parenting through positive reinforcement is far easier than letting your children experience the negative consequences of their actions.Truthfully, it does not require finances to do so.Rewarding your children can be as easy as a hug, a high five, or an 'ata boy!'The next level might be letting your child pick what meal the family eats and following through.Some parents we know turn everything into a reward- from TV time to special nights with mom or dad.Is it not better to 'have to' spend an evening in the park with one of your children because that was the reward she chose for her good behavior rather than spending an evening making sure she stays on her bed doing nothing because she did something wrong?Deep down, you know what is right for your kids.Most of the time, we know the right thing to do.We, as parents, just have to do it.

Most of all in this process, we have to remember that parenting has to be proactive.Consequences must be predetermined.If your child does not know the result of their action, then what you do is punish them.This means, at times, new offenses come up that must be discussed before consequences can be put in place.Do yourself a favor and stop feeling as if your child 'got away with it.'Life is full of examples of people of whom we would say that, 'she got her just deserves.'Typically this is said because the general impression people had was that this person had somehow averted the consequences of her actions up, and to, that point.This being said, there are some 'new' offenses that our children know are wrong before they do them.Sometimes we must assume the consequences in order for our children to understand the problem with the negative action they took.

Ultimately, we have to set the table for them.'If you _____ (cause) then you will receive _____ (effect).This sentence can read, 'If you **hit your sister**, then you will

spend the rest of the night in your room, sans entertainment.' However, this sentence can also read, 'If you **read five books cover to cover,** then **we will go out for dinner and ice cream- your choice**!'This empowers your children to choose right over wrong.Most of us find it difficult to do the wrong thing (hitting your sister), while we are doing the right thing (reading books).This also empowers your children to be individuals, free from the pressures of the crowd.You are not making their choices for them- they are.All it takes is a whole lot of consistency...

...And that, most of all, with follow through.If you do not follow through, you have simply threatened your child.Remember telling someone you were mad at, 'that's not a threat, that's a promise?'As a parent it always has to be a promise.So choose your battles carefully and make sure that big consequences are matched to equally big offenses.To do anything less will show you quickly, as a parent, just how smart your children are.After all, if forgetting to take out the trash and beating up your sister exact the same consequence, why not get the 'bang for your buck' and give the sibling a beat down?**If the volcano erupts for a pebble, you might as well throw a boulder**.

Be reminded that ultimately, reinforcing good behavior is your greatest 'disciplinary' ally.Your child has a felt need for attention and, like we said before, she will willingly take sour milk over no milk at all.What she considers most nutritious to her soul will be obvious to you.All you have to do is be a Student of your child.

Chapter 22: Building Resilient Children

re·sil·iencenounability to recover readily from illness, depression, adversity, or the like.

The American Academy of Pediatrics advises parents that building resilience in children is one of the most significant things you can do to ensure long-term emotional health and success in adulthood. Resilient children get sad, but can bounce back from challenging feelings without wallowing in them, and your behavior strongly influences how resilient your child becomes.

No matter how hard you try to protect your kids from the negative effects of divorce, they are going to have to deal with complicated emotions and ongoing challenges. From missing one parent, to having to split up birthdays and holidays, even the best divorce is challenging for children.

Creating Confidence

A confident child is a resilient child. Confident children know they can navigate the challenges of life. Some ideas for building confidence include:

Giving your child access to a wide range of hobbies – reading, sports, art, music, etc. -- so that she can discover her own strengths.

Praising your child for effort rather than achievement. Child Psychologist Albert Bandura developed the concept of **self-efficacy** to characterize children who trusted their own abilities. He found that children with high self-efficacy understood that achievement was the result of effort, not innate skill.

Allowing your child to fail, and certainly not punishing him when he does.

Scaffolding your child. Scaffolding is the process of giving a child assistance to do something he couldn't otherwise do on his own, without doing it for him. For example, if your child is trying to write a sentence, rather than spelling the words for him or telling him how to write the sentence, try helping him sound out the words.

Positive Coping Strategies

Children need to learn positive coping skills such as relying on friends, exercising or playing instead of yelling, and seeking help when they need it. Although your child shouldn't see you as weak or in need of her help, if she knows that you sometimes struggle with your emotions, she'll learn that it's ok for her to do the same. For example, if you've had a frustrating day at work, let your child watch you take a few minutes to mull it over or exercise. And when she has a tough day, encourage her to do something she loves, to call a friend, or to take a brief time-out in her room.

Encourage her to talk about her emotions, and never criticize her for her feelings. If your child is having trouble managing her emotions, don't be afraid to get professional help. Early intervention when your child is struggling can protect her from more serious long-term problems.

Connection and Community

It truly does take a village to raise a child, and if you try to do it all on your own, you're compromising your child's resilience. Encourage her to develop strong relationships with grandparents, aunts, uncles, siblings, and cousins, and give her plenty of opportunities to spend time with loving adults. As your child gets older, he may rely on these adults when he's afraid of coming to you. Similarly, honor your child's friendships by making playdates and giving him alone time with his friends. Children frequently rely on their friends to provide emotional support, and building strong social skills is a key for adult success.

Control

Children live in a world controlled by adults, and children whose parents are divorcing frequently, feel like they have no control over their own lives. Giving your child some control over her own life can help her build resilience, and will help her gain the problem-solving skills she needs to thrive in adulthood. This doesn't mean you should give up on parenting her. Instead, give her simple choices. For example, ask her whether she'd rather eat dinner now or in an hour. If your children are older, solicit their input about your custody arrangement. For example, ask them whether they'd rather have longer periods of time with each parent by, for example, spending a month with mom and a month with dad, or if they'd prefer to go back and forth more frequently.

Giving your child a sense of control also means choosing your battles. Fighting over an article of her clothing or the sport he plays are recipes for making your child feel like his or her emotions don't matter. Instead, ask your child about her feelings and honor her opinions, even when they differ from your own.

Chapter 23: Teenage Sex And Contraception

Are you still there?Are you hiding?Come on out now...!If there is one thing that sends a loving mother or father completely insane it is the thought that their precious darling might be indulging in a – shock horror - physical relationship!The temptation to sweep such possibilities so far under the rug they will never be seen or heard of again is almost irresistible.Unfortunately, turning a blind eye to one's teenager's sexual urges can result in the direst of consequences for everyone.

Coming from a family of close-mouthed, inhibited and emotional wrecks it was easy to see how a teenager could go completely off the rails.With no one to confide in and no one to help source those all-important contraceptives young kids with an urge to indulge in the physical side of affection will go to almost any lengths to find their own solutions.And this includes not taking any precautions whatever against pregnancy and sexually transmitted infections.

In a world where mothers think nothing of vaccinating their children against a plethora of diseases that could result in permanent scarring it is ridiculous that the same parents allow their children to dabble in unprotected sex with the possibility that it could ruin their education, their prospects, their career and wipe out just about every aspiration they ever had - simply because mum is too embarrassed to talk about sex and contraception.

To a degree schools and colleges – not to mention the bike sheds – play their parts in sex education.The best institutional tuition includes discussion groups on how sexual behaviour affects other areas of adult life and the emotional side of being 'involved'; the dangers of casual sex and the consequences of unprotected sex.The worst treatment of the subject is a cursory and clinical observation of the facts accompanied by a series of detached and emotionless diagrams that have little to do with the impact the sexual act can impose on work, study and family life.

Nobody in their right mind would welcome the opportunity to discuss their sex life with their parents!Are you nuts?! It is not a subject that comes easily over the dinner table unless it is bandied around siblings in a wink-wink-nudge-nudge-leg-pulling session.This is fine and harmless but cannot take the place of a gentle but frank and straight forward talk on a one-to-one basis to let your teenager understand how you feel about it; how you think he or she should go about getting sexual protection; how **they** feel about it and an in-depth discussion on what the possible consequences are of neglecting one's sexual health.

While you are on the subject, clear up the rules of the house when it comes to inviting boyfriends or girlfriends home for some hanky-panky.People have their own feelings and limitations when it comes to allowing their 'child' to have guests of the opposite sex stay overnight in their 'child's' bedroom.Whatever your thoughts are on this issue, make them clear from the outset.

The modern world has had an influence on the way in which parents approach the issue of their kids having sex under their roof.The dangers of finding an alternative location for sexual activity are obvious and scary enough to make many parents put aside their own reservations and allow a measure of permissiveness.It's up to you but remember that your disallowing sex under your roof will not prevent it taking place – think about that before you send your kid's sex life 'underground'.

When it comes to contraception there are dozens of opportunities to combat the possibilities of pregnancy and there is certainly no excuse for being 'stuck' with an unwanted pregnancy providing religion and moral considerations are kept out of it.

A Range of Goodies

The method of contraception usually chosen by teenagers is the barrier method which of course protects against pregnancy and also sexually transmitted diseases.Male condoms, female condoms and gel or foam spermicides are all in prolific use.All of it comes under the heading of good stuff as far as responsible parents are concerned.

A number of young girls opt for the oral contraceptive pill.Many experience side effects and far too many girls make early experiments with their periods which hitherto might be incredibly inconvenient but which now may be controlled by manipulating their pill dosage.This can lead to problems later so advise your daughter that indulging in this practice needs to be under the strict guidance of her GP.

It is important to make your daughter understand that the pill will provide a 90% plus protection against pregnancy but is no use whatever as a barrier against infection.If your daughter wants to start taking the pill, she must also realise a condom is still required.

The first step, at least for girls when it comes to contraception, is a visit to the doctor.If your family doctor feels a little uncomfortable then do not stand in the way of your daughter seeking advice from a family planning clinic or doctor of her choice.It does not matter as long as she is seen and properly advised, given all of the options available.

Do not accompany your daughter on this trip unless you are expressly invited to do so.As much as you are concerned for her welfare, getting her this far is your job – from here she can expect to have some privacy.The chances are she will talk to you about this anyway but do not intrude. If she is old enough to sleep with boys she is old enough to manage her contraception sensibly as long as she is in possession of all the facts regarding risks and consequences of neglecting to use timely and adequate protection.Taking this 'step back' from your daughter's private world is usually deeply appreciated and will result in your daughter sharing information with you.If she does not, it is unproductive (excuse the pun) to press her confidence.She will, more than likely, clam up and who could blame her?This is her body and her first step into an adult world where privacy in such things must be respected and if they are not they should be!

There is a deal of difference between privacy and secrecy.Should you discover contraceptives in your daughter's (or son's) room the last thing you should do is blunder down the stairs two at a time, waving a pack of condoms like a parade banner to inform the extended family your darling baby has been sleeping around.No, no, no…

Think about your reactions to your teenager's new found maturity and ask yourself which scenario is more acceptable: a physical relationship, albeit without your knowledge but at least with protection against pregnancy and disease, or a spontaneous and hurried encounter in the back of a car somewhere without adequate precautions?

Do you think that when you are in your dying throes you will reflect on the bad decisions of your life and think that you should have made your teenager wait another two years to have sex?Unlikely...

Despite all the instruction and advice you give there is always the possibility that your teenager will be the one to become pregnant while still at school.If the unthinkable does happen there is a time and place for recriminations, sorrow and anger.Once the shock and horror has edge into the background there must be a practical discussion on what is to happen next.

You will need to remember that your daughter's pregnancy brings all the usual uncomfortable symptoms of expecting a baby and these must be considered carefully no matter how much you would like to yell and shout and throw things around the room.Go visit a friend if you have to do that but take care not to distress your pregnant daughter.

There are a number of options open for girls who have unexpectedly become pregnant and these include termination, adoption or welcoming the new baby into the family:all of the choices are hard to face for a mum who might have wished a different year ahead for her daughter.Take it in your stride and try to address each decision calmly, all the while remembering that this is your daughter's ultimate call.Supporting what you believe to be a bad decision is the hardest part of parenting teenagers.They do not always come up with the right decisions but of course unless you provide emotional and moral support there is likely to be none aboard.Remember that before you withdraw your help or place pressure on your daughter to do 'the right thing' – the usual euphemism for doing what YOU want her to do.

For families experiencing the difficulties of teenage pregnancy there is always the possibility that a second adult might wish to be welcomed into the home – the expectant father.This can cause a number of headaches, many of them financial if the boy has no job or is still studying or comes from a family you cannot approve of.

In today's broken economy there are always practical difficulties to solve when it comes to accommodating young kids who are expectant parents themselves.The housing ladder is no longer an option for many youngsters and living with mum and dad or with grandparents is the only way forward.

The pattern of modern life has changed enormously in the past fifty years.There was a time when young families expected to live independently – now it is accepted that they live at home and contribute financially to the household expenses.When everyone is considerate toward everyone else all is peace and harmony but there is usually one of the fold who drives everyone else up the wall.These things are sent to try us – keep calm and carry on!

Bad Habits

Smoking is rife in the modern age despite the efforts of health experts that confirm smoking will give you cancer and shorten your life.Teenagers are as tempted by the offer of a cigarette today as they were when it first became fashionable.Although parents often identify their kid has been smoking they neglect to do anything about it thinking it is a 'phase' and their kid will get over it when the novelty wears off.

The novelty will not wear off and in fact the longer your child smokes the harder it will be to give it up. Stop it as soon as possible.

Soft drugs are also popular and marijuana is legal in certain parts of the world.In other places its use is largely ignored as long as consumers use it privately.Tolerating the use of marijuana is unacceptable.It is not 'harmless' despite press to the contrary and in fact cause paranoia and introvert behaviour.Sort it out early to avoid bigger problems later on. If you cannot stop your kid using soft drugs, seek advice from local community support groups that have the resources and expertise to help.

Chapter 24: Parenting Styles

The Nurturing Parent Model

There are many different styles of parenting. Overwhelmed new and prospective parents may be understandably trying to decide which the best style to use is, and which will generate the best results for themselves and for their children. They may be unsure of whom to trust for advice in an era where we are bombarded with information about everything. Fortunately, parenting and child growth and development is well-trod ground in psychology and other areas. Good parenting represents a range of behavior, rather than a protocol of essential directives. The two extremes that parents can fall into include being overly strict, and overly permissive. Parents fall into these two extremes largely out of fear, a desire for control, and a difficult time moderating their own behavior.

Strict and Permissive Parenting

Strict parents enforce rules, often with harsh punishments, and demand firm obedience from their children. They will often appeal to their own authority as parents when their children ask questions about why certain rules are in place. The 'we're the parents and we say so' cliché is strictly planted in this 'strict parent' model. As is the similar cliché: 'as long as you live under my house, you obey my rules.' The crucial underlying factor is that they do not engage with their children's feelings on the matter, and they do not explain why certain rules are in place. They place emphasis on family hierarchies and the 'order of things.'

Permissive parents represent the other extreme. They avoid giving their children any limits at all. They do not enforce any real rules on their children, or else, enforce them insufficiently. Essentially, they are partly shifting the burden of raising children onto the children themselves.

Reasons behind Certain Parenting Styles

Strict parents may believe that unless they impose a very firm hand in exactly the way they are doing it, their children will never do as they say. In short, they may believe that their way is the only way. Strict parents may believe that getting their children's perspective on any given problem means giving up power, and ultimately losing control of their children. They are modeling the parent/child relationship as a combatant power struggle. Stern behavior is absolutely warranted during tense, immediate emergencies. If your child is about to approach on open flame, wander too close to a moving vehicle, or is in any other imminently threatening situation, parents should not worry about whether they were too stern in the heat of the moment. Not only will parents barely have time to even react in such a situation, their stern behavior will do more good than harm. The important thing is how you treat them after the event, when they will no doubt be crying and asking for support. Strict parents may make the mistake of continuing to see the situation as an emergency that demands rash action, rather than an opportunity for education and mutual understanding.

Permissive parents may be reacting against having been raised in a strict parent family themselves. They may focus too much on being their children's friends. They may be concerned about the long-term affects any discipline may have on their children, and may not see any middle ground between harsh discipline and none whatsoever. While strict parents may deny all necessary agencies to their children, permissive parents may be giving their children the same agency as adults. Children do have different needs than adults, and it is important for all parents to understand how best to accommodate them. Indeed, permissive parents may worry about even being stern during dire emergencies, and may resist their own urges to appropriately intervene. Some people may believe that whether parents are strict or permissive is based on the nature of their parental punishments. That is to say, strict parents spank their children and more permissive parents just give them 'time outs,' and other less physical forms of discipline.

In fact, both forms of punishment could work as part of a strict parent model, and they both have the effect of children being conditioned to do what the parent wants as a means of regulating their behavior. Either way, children do not form an independent basis for making moral decisions any- where near as easily as with a nurturing parent model. Finding a middle ground between strict and permissive parenting can prove challenging for many parents. Having certain ideals or guiding principles is important for everyone when embarking on any task. Putting those ideals into practice in every situation is challenging. Communicating with children is often different from communicating with adults, and children cannot be expected to be as reasonable as adults. Learning to deal with your own frustrations when interacting with children during tense moments while setting standards in the healthiest way is part of learning how to be a parent.

Inductive Discipline

One of the most valuable things any parent can do is not only imposing rules on children, but explains the reasons behind rules. Parents should not automatically assume that their children will not understand the reasons behind rules, and therefore they should not even try to explain them. Nurturing parents should try to reason with their children. They can explain why something a child did was negative, how it hurts other people, and why people should not behave that way. If parents are indeed instilling good values in their children, all of their standards should have good explanations behind them. Strict parents rarely care about their children's feelings on any given matter, thinking children are supposed to obey them in all circumstances.

Permissive parents may place too much of a value on how children feel moment to moment, without truly thinking about why children feel certain things. Nurturing parents ask their children what they are feeling, and try to get them to think about why they think and feel that way. All people are more likely to consider your feelings when you consider theirs. Using a high level of empathy to try to figure out why kids are behaving a certain way, and then talking to them about it, can make problem-solving seem more like a negotiation and less like a battle of wills.

Nurturing parents do not ignore their children's misbehavior, unlike permissive parents. They also do not bribe them in order to motivate them to comply with their parents' wishes. Unlike strict parents, they do not regularly yell at their children, or withdraw affection as a form of punishment. Reasoning with children is referred to as inductive discipline, and its benefits have been quite well documented. The nurturing parent model has a multitude of advantages in how it influences children's growth and development. Children learn to empathize with other people more effectively as parents explain the reasons behind certain actions, and how they and their children think and feel. It also encourages children to see their actions in a broader context, outside themselves, which is very important for any junior member of society.

As much as new parents may fear 'lecturing' their children, ultimately, they will have to find some way of communicating about their standards for their children's behavior. The reasons behind rules and standards may seem obvious to them, but it is every bit as obvious as all the other things children must learn from an early age. Some parents may be more likely to favor negative reinforcement over punishment. In negative reinforcement, parents give their children rewards for good behavior, and take away those rewards for bad behavior. Unlike bribery, which involves giving a child a reward in advance, negative reinforcement involves rewards in response to other stimuli. Say you have gotten your daughter a bicycle because she did well in school. You would then take it away if she then performed poorly.

One of the fundamentals of society is that people feel well when they do good things, and feel badly when they do bad things. People are less likely to do good things when they do not feel any special incentive. However, parents should avoid using affection as a means of punishment and reward. Negative reinforcement works much better than simple punishment. The strict parent model values discipline, obedience, and a strong work ethic. The permissive parent model values undirected personal growth and freedom. The nurturing parent model values responsibility, empathy, and mutual respect. Nurturing parents prepare children for far more walks of life than strict or permissive ones, who are both asking children to fend for themselves, albeit in opposite directions. Nurturing parents help children interact with a larger society in a more healthy way.

Chapter 25: Escaping The Madness

Every parent is entitled to "me" time. Just every once in a while you need to break free. The mistake that many parents make is losing touch with friends outside of the family circle. You make your life a lot happier if you are able to keep in touch with people that matter to you and your kids won't mind you going out to enjoy yourself. In fact, they will see how much happier this makes you as a human being. If you plan a night out, this can be together or with your friends, then make sure that the kids have a babysitter for the night. If you try to keep weekends free for the family, this can happen any evening of the week and may just give you something to look forward to.

The kind of madness you can expect to experience as a parent, you will already be aware of. Sometimes you feel so isolated from adult company. Sometimes you feel like you are talking to the wall because the kids are not taking any notice of you. Sometimes you feel like your needs are being left behind in favor of the kids' needs and that's not right. Just as you respect and love your kids, encourage them to love and respect you. Show the kids the fancy outfit you are going to wear. Plan with them what they are going to do while you are out. Make sure that the family is treated as an open forum where things like this can be discussed openly. You may find that your little girl loves to see her mommy dressed up ready to go out or that your son likes to see dad all dressed up to go out into the forest with his buddies. As the children grow, encourage them to meet you for meals in town and allow them to have their own level of independence.

Permissions and Privileges

The worst feeling in the world for a kid is that a parent doesn't care or that a parent doesn't believe the child. When you check on where your child is going this weekend, don't do so accusingly. Do so with love. Show your child that it's a normal thing for you to check up to see if your child is going to a safe environment. You are going to get teens who lie to you. You are going to get smaller kids who go to places you told them not to go, but you need to have a pattern to your behavior so that the kids know what the penalties are for lying.

If you child considered him/herself as an adult, then explain that you expect adult behavior and that until that happens, they will be treated as children. If you worry about where your kids are going, make it a point from a very early age to always know where your kids are. If you establish this while they are young, then teens won't expect anything different and will expect to be accountable. The privileges that your kid is allowed are conditional upon behaving in a set way. As long as those rules are made clear from the start, the child should expect to lose privileges if they betray your trust.

Your Escape

There are other ways of escaping than simply going out. Sometimes you just want peace and quiet in your own home. Maybe, as a couple, you want a romantic evening without the kids. That's when relatives come in very handy indeed. You may want to do hobbies that require silence. Try to create yourself a space in the home where kids don't go. This can be used for art, for reading, for meditation or whatever it is that you want to do, but the children need to understand that, just like their bedrooms, this is a space where you can go when you want to do your own hobbies and the kids need to respect that.

Perhaps you want to chill out for an evening on your own and simply have a movie night for the girls or a sports night for the boys. If this is the case, then try to get family members to take the kids to give you that freedom. I think that the best investment you can make when you have kids is in the people who will help you to escape when you need to. Perhaps you have neighbors with kids of around the same age that you know and trust to take over looking after your kids for an evening in exchange for you looking after theirs at another time. All of these give and take relationships really do help you in times when you need that escape route. Your kids don't benefit from you being overtired and grouchy. You don't benefit from the kids being over tired and grouchy. Learn to take time off. You are entitled to it and should not feel that you are letting your kids down when you choose to use this option.

When you find yourself needing to get away, even a drive to the beach or a drive into town on your own can help. Sometimes all you want is to be somewhere else. As long as you can rely upon people around you, you have this escape option and it's not bad parenting. Your kids gain from your absence because they learn to be less dependent on having you there all of the time and they also learn to socialize with others which is always healthy.

Chapter 26: Visitations And Divorce

Most courts want both parents to be equally involved the parenting of the children after a divorce. Working out visitations can sometime be difficult and may take some time for the children to adjust. Start by discussing what works best for each parent and then devise a calendar as a means of tracking the dates so no one gets confused or forgets. The schedules should work for the parents as well as the children. Take under consideration the activities that the children maybe involved in or conflicts that work schedules may impose. If parents fail to agree on a workable visitation schedule then courts will have to get involved. This may result in a stricter visitation schedules because courts generally will switch the holidays each year with each parent to make it as fair as possible. They will make exceptions for Mother's Day and Father's Day allowing the children to spend the day with the parent that fits that category.

When children miss out on social gatherings with their friends due to having to go with the other parent it can become tiresome and frustrating for them. There are also events that the children may have to miss while with the other parent such as reunions, vacations etc. It's not possible to schedule all of these events around the visitation schedules of the divorced couple. If a parent is willing to be accommodating then they will give up some of their parenting time for the benefit of their children so they can attend such events. This should be a two sided street though with both parents being willing to compromise. Such flexibility when it comes to the visitation schedules can suddenly make the children feel a lot happier. Make sure that you are not taking advantage of the ex-spouses willingness to accommodate scheduling conflicts. Make sure the children understand that that you can't always change your visitations with them to allow them to attend other events.If both parents are very reasonable then the visitation process should work out for everyone involved.

Being A Quality Parent When Living In A Different City

Sometimes after a divorce one of the parents may find it is necessary to relocate to get away from the many memories or to start a new job.Distance should not hemp your ability to be a quality parent.Make an effort to instill into the children that you did not move to get away from them because to many children blame themselves for the divorce. Sit and talk with your children and explain why you are moving and that you will always be accessible to them day or night. Make sure that they have phone numbers including home, cell and work.If phone charges are a problem for the children then get them a pre-paid phone.

Always show an interest in what your children are doing particularly at school and other outside activities.Ask about their friends and how they interact together. A computer with a web cam is a fantastic way to visit. Also you can send recent pictures of each other. Email allows you to sent chat on a regular basis. Remember to send personal card on special occasions like birthdays. Make an extra effort to schedule time with the children either by traveling to their city or have them to come and visit you. Be considerate in working out holidays and spring break.

It may be more cost effective for you to travel to where they are at then it will be to bring them to you. It depends on how far away you are and how many children you have. The ages of the children matters too as younger ones often have a difficult time traveling. Most airlines do allow older children to fly alone but this can be hard for parents to accept. Never get in the habit of feeling that the only way to show love when you live far away is to send expensive gifts. Your children need to fell that you love them and that you care about them regardless of how many miles are between you and them.

Ex-Spouse Doesn't Want To See The Children After A Divorce

In most cases divorcees fight to see their children as much as possible; however, there are instances when a person does not want to have anything to do with the children after the divorce. It can be difficult when the ex-spouse doesn't want to see the children after a divorce, but some people are happy with the arrangement. Sometimes the resentment over the divorce may make an ex-spouse want to start over with a brand new life. Other times it may be a matter of psychological problems that prevent them from caring for the children.

Some parents may feel it is in the best interest of the children to stay primarily with one or the other for whatever the reason. Another reason is one of the spouses maybe involved with a person that does not want children around.The children can be severely hurt by these types of scenarios and may begin to blame themselves for the parent removing themselves from their lives.This is a discussion you need to have with your children but keep in mind that how you handle the situation is going to affect them. Do not make excuses for the missing spouse but try to effectively communicate without blaming the absent parent; explain as much as you can that it isn't their fault their parent doesn't want to see them at this time.. Your openness and honesty will help them put these types of issues in prospective and let them know that you respect their feelings. Hopefully, this will also reduce any resentment the children maybe holding against the missing in action parent.You may say something like the ex-spouse is trying to focus on getting their life on track so try to be patient and understand. While it isn't fair that this responsibility falls on your shoulders you need to take care of it for the sake of your children.

Should Siblings Remain Together After A Divorce?

Children have their ups and downs with each other, but you will find in tough times they often depend on each another. That leads to the question of siblings being together when a couple gets divorced. Sometimes it isn't that simple, such as when one child doesn't biologically belong to both parents. Most times couples agree to have the siblings all remain together because it's easier on both spouses that way.The world of siblings can become very scary when they are faced with the possibility of being separated from each other. No one beside the siblings knows what they are feeling and they need to feel as if they can talk to someone. In some cases the spouses make a decision to separate the siblings which can be hard for the parents but even harder for the siblings who have come to depend upon each other.

Parents should make sure they aren't influencing the children's decision as to which parent they would like to reside with. They should be made to feel as if they can change their mind if they desire to do so. If one the children reside with a parent that has to relocate out of town then they may want the child to remain in school with the other parent particularly if there is only a year or two left of high school. If that is not agreeable then try to let the child remain until the school year is finished. Parents are sometime forced to separate the siblings because of finances and inadequate living accommodations. When children are very young they may need to remain with their mother for a variety of reasons. Older children have the flexibility of being able to travel alone to see their parents while the your one's are solely dependent on their parents to transport them.

If any of the children has special needs then this presents a different type of problem since they may require needs and care that are too complex or costly to have in both locations. This may result in one parent being fully responsible for that particular child. It depends on the abilities of the parents as well as the severity of the medical problems that the child has. The decision to keep siblings together after a divorce is a decision that each family will have to assess. Separating the siblings may work well for some issues at hand but not for others.Regardless of the decision, all of the children need to know that they have the love and encouragement of both parents.

Chapter 27: What Factors Influence The Parenting Philosophy Of Parent?

Parents have many influential philosophies and influences how parents deal with issues such as gender roles and discipline. Some parents have a less rigid approach while others have an ideal in their mind. "It is a good idea to understand what children expect from parent and what goals are for a child (Chen, et al., 1998)". To develop a philosophy parents should consider their children and their temperament and motivation.

6.1. Family roots

Family of origin has a strong influence on the type of parenting. "Many beliefs, values, habits and thought patterns are rooted in family life before". People are able to be parents differently than they were parented and taught lessons on how to be a parent. Reflecting the positive and negative aspects of how they were created and developing own philosophy of parenting can help parents in setting goals because parents often have different parenting experiences. "Family Education suggests that it is important for partners to talk through their parenting ideals" (Smenyak, 2015).

6.2. Religious Beliefs

Parenting philosophies can be affected by having a religion or no religion. Parents who need a priority list often contains these religious beliefs of their parents. There are regulations and rules on family life in religious families, which reflect the church and the family rules are often built in the presence of the influence of church. Families with strong religious ties can create the perfect family from other sources. "Sometimes parents bring experience and religious beliefs in the family, even if they are not active in a church or faith" (Smenyak, 2015).

6.3. Social Influences

Some philosophies of parenting were created in the name of the parenting communities. Examples are: "attachment parenting, which aims to create strong emotional ties; slow parenting, which encourages parents to not over plan and organize their children's lives" , and parenting for all those who believe in the dignity and sense of dignity of child (Smenyak, 2015). "Parents can find their own parenting styles influenced by their peers. Sometimes a particular philosophy becomes popular" in different parenting styles of a community group or school.

Chapter 28: Bully Strategies: Teach Your Child How To Deal With Bullies

Bullying is a serious problem; a recent survey showed that about 22 percent of all children fall prey to it. This means it is likely your child might be suffering from this problem at school, which is why it is imperative that you teach your child strategies to deal with bullies. In order to do this you need to:

Notice Your Child's Behavior: Begin by observing your child's mood and behavior after school. If you find your child feeling scared, uninterested in things, and lost all the time, then it might be due to the bullying at school, or outside of home. If that is the case, talk to your child and assure him or her of your support. It may take your child a while to open up, so be patient and do not push your child.

Find out the bullying type: Once your child confides in you, find out what type of bullying your child is experiencing. Is it verbal (spoken abuse), physical (assault), relational (covert or mean girl bullying) and cyber (online) bullying? After you have figured out the type, you teach your child effective strategies to deal with each type accordingly.

Bully Strategies

Verbal Bullying

Tell your child to approach the authorities so that the authorities acknowledge the existence of bullying in the school. Next, teach your child to use positive self-talk to affirm thoughts that he or she can face the bully. Once your child is strong enough for that, your child should maintain direct eye contact with the bully and look the bully directly in the eye. Tell your child to walk confidently and speak firmly when the bully approaches him or her. This tactic works well for most bullies; however, if the bullying does subside, teach your child to use fogging or comeback lines. Fogging is when your child responds to the bully using neutral or agreeing statements.

For example, if a bully tells your child that he looks weird, your child should say, 'Who cares?' or 'yeah, I know, so what's your problem?' Comeback lines are statements that help increase confidence.

Physical Bullying

All the strategies for dealing with verbal bullying will work here too, but you should also teach your child how to make a strong, bold move such as hitting the bully if he or she does not stop bullying your child. Once a bully knows your child can respond back the same way, he or she will quit tormenting your child.

Relational Bullying

The best way for your child to deal with bullies who practice mean girl bullying is to teach your child how to detach him or herself from such people, and engage in healthy activities.

Cyber Bullying

To stop cyber bullying, make sure your child confides in you or another trustworthy person. Also, teach your child how to set difficult passwords for online accounts. In case, the bullying gets worse, you might have to get the law involved.

Chapter 29: Always Have A Reason

We always become our parents to some extent.One place where this is almost universally true is some of the things we do and say to our kids.

We all grow up vowing to never yell at our kids or say "because I told you so" as a reason for doing something.Well, unless you are a living saint (there are a few) you will get frustrated and yell and you will say things like "just be quiet and do it."I know, it's a little depressing but it is a fact.

Now, sometimes, you are going to be wrong, you'll get frustrated when you shouldn't, accuse a kid of breaking a dish that they actually did not break.Sometimes it really was her brother.When that happens, don't be afraid to say that you're sorry.Some people will say that this is a sign of weakness, that it will undermine your authority as a parent.

I strongly disagree. Nothing undermines your authority more than your kids learning that you don't listen to them, that you are arrogant and prideful or even stupid.Those are just some of the bad lessons that your children can learn from you being obstinate.

Admitting you're wrong and saying sorry shows both strength and compassion.That's how the kids learn the importance of learning from their mistakes and that it is possible to recover from them.

Even though you will say silly things like "because I said so," more than once it is still important to have a reason.Ideally you'll have that reason at the ready when they ask why they have to clean their room or take the dog for a walk but that just isn't always the case.

There will be times that you have three people talking to you at once while trying to fix the sink and a quickly barked "just do as I said" is the quickest way to move things along.But later, your son and daughter will ask why again.They are little philosophers after all.

Have your reason at the ready, or at least have one developed when you are explaining to your child why you don't want her to do or not do something.My oldest has been big on getting a cellphone for a few months now. Being that she is in middle school it doesn't seem like she needs one.

When she asks why, citing the ever popular "all my friends have one" as a rationale, I make sure to respond with answers like "it's a distraction you don't need," and "they cost money every month."And she does get it. She doesn't like it, but that's okay.

That actually is another thing, your kids will not always like everything you tell them to do, whether it is to eat her spinach or hang out with his baby sister, your kids are likely to grumble about it just a bit.

Personally, this doesn't bother me.So long as they are not disrespectful, I have no problem with them voicing their opinion so long as things get done.Besides I don't expect my kids to like taking care of the dishes.But the dishes surely aren't going to take care of themselves either.

Conclusion

Being a parent is very challenging as no child comes with a manual on what you can do and what not to do. So, basically, you will need to know more about your child in order to know how best to nurture them to become smart children. This requires effort, patience and perseverance. However, you will be glad that you did what you did to ensure that they turned out pretty okay.

www.ingramcontent.com/pod-product-compliance
Lightning Source LLC
Chambersburg PA
CBHW072009070526
44583CB00015B/1407